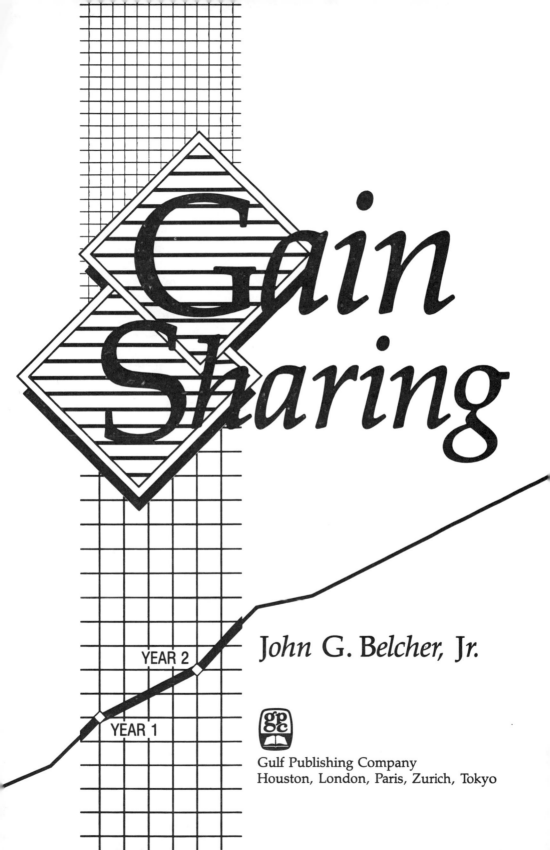

Gain Sharing

John G. Belcher, Jr.

gpc

Gulf Publishing Company
Houston, London, Paris, Zurich, Tokyo

Gain Sharing

Gulf Publishing Company
Book Division
P.O. Box 2608, Houston, Texas 77252-2608

10   9   8   7   6   5   4   3   2   1

**Library of Congress Cataloging-in-Publication
Data**

Belcher, John G.
    Gain sharing : the new path to
    profits and productivity /
John G. Belcher, Jr.
        p.   cm.
    Includes index.
    ISBN 0-87201-324-3
    Gain sharing.   2. Gain sharing—United States.
    I. Title.
HD4928.G34B45   1991
658.3'225—dc20   91-15351
                                                      CIP

Dedication

To the source of my personal rewards:
Nancy, Scott, and Stephen

Contents

Introduction

While gain sharing programs were hard to find ten or fifteen years ago, their use is growing rapidly in industry today. This growth is not an isolated incident, but reflects fundamental changes that are taking place on the American business scene.

American business is at a watershed in its history, as the role of management undergoes a painful transition. The old model, which dates back to the Industrial Revolution, is slowly but surely fading away. The challenges of global competition will no longer allow managers to treat workers as faceless cogs in a machine, to be directed and controlled. Companies can no longer afford to have uninformed, uninvolved, and uncommitted employees. Cumbersome, bureaucratic organizations with systems and practices that are designed to minimize the role and impact of people will not succeed in a global economy characterized by rapid changes and the emergence of ever tougher competition.

The transition to a new, more viable form of management is essential to the long-term health of the American economy and the survival of today's business enterprises. Fortunately, this transition is taking place. The change cannot be fully effected, however, with our traditional reward systems in place. We simply cannot forge a new culture with pay systems that were designed in a different era, under a different set of management assumptions.

Gain sharing grows apace as more and more managers begin to appreciate the role of reward systems in supporting and reinforcing employee involvement. Gain sharing meets today's business needs and is indeed a system whose time has come.

Any system that offers great potential for meeting business imperatives can be misused, however. There is, for example, a growing tendency for companies that do not meet basic readiness criteria to rush headlong into gain sharing. And lack of knowledge about gain sharing system design often leads to plans that do not adequately reflect business priorities or contain fatal design flaws.

The purpose of this book is to provide the reader with a thorough grounding in the principles of gain sharing. To the extent that it succeeds in that objective, the reader will be better able to judge whether gain sharing makes sense for his or her business. Perhaps even more importantly, the reader will have an appreciation for the importance of good system design and will be better equipped to create a customized gain sharing program that creatively meets the unique needs of the business.

John G. Belcher, Jr.
Houston, Texas

Chapter 1

Gain Sharing and Today's Business Environment

"The future ain't what it used to be."

—Yogi Berra

The 1990s may well be remembered by business historians as a decade of change. While change has always been a fact of life for American businesses, the transformation of the competitive environment in the years leading up to the last decade of the twentieth century has been truly extraordinary. Asian nations developed formidable competitive machines that decimated some of our premier industries. Consumers have rebelled against poor quality, and companies have been forced to refocus on the customer. Deregulation has transformed stable and secure industries into maelstroms of cutthroat competition. The good old days of stable markets and gradual change are gone; never before has the ability to adapt to change been more important to business success, if not to survival itself.

The savvy companies, recognizing the magnitude of the challenge presented by a global economy, more demanding customers and more rapid change, have begun to evaluate and challenge the assumptions underlying their management systems, processes, and practices. There is a growing recognition that our tried, true, and traditional ways of managing the organization are not effective in today's business environment. They were, after all, designed for a different era.

The tremendous increase in interest in employee involvement or participative management is a manifestation of this felt need to

1

change. For decades, jobs and organizational systems were designed to minimize the impact of the human resource. Frederick Taylor taught management to design jobs "scientifically" in order to remove worker discretion from the job activity and ensure maximum efficiency. Communications were largely on a "need-to-know" basis, and supervisors learned to manage autocratically. The message sent by management to employees was clear: people are of little value and must be controlled in order to minimize their impact.

While these practices seemed appropriate in an environment of low competition, stability, and steady economic growth, they have side effects that are devastating in today's era of global competition. Uncommitted and uninformed employees neither understand nor care about the business challenges facing the enterprise. Low self-esteem lessens workers' pride in their work and results in poor quality. With jobs standardized and formal policies and procedures entrenched, there is little adaptability to changes in markets, customer demands, or business conditions. The extra layers of management and specialists required to adequately control the organization produces an unwieldy, cumbersome, and costly organizational structure. How can businesses compete under these circumstances with organizations who have highly committed, highly involved employees?

Participative management then, is simply a manifestation of business adapting to change. By creating management practices that allow companies to maximize, rather than minimize, the contribution of an important resource (their people), they significantly improve the organization's ability to meet world-class standards of cost and quality and to respond to the never-ending competitive challenges of a global economy.

These and other related changes are necessary, and those companies that have the courage and commitment to initiate and follow through with fundamental changes in their management practices will be rewarded with greater stability, more committed employees, and higher profits in these turbulent times.

However, the transformation will be incomplete (and in fact may ultimately fail) if management does not attack one of its most critical systems—the reward system. A company cannot hope to institutionalize a non-traditional management philosophy and work culture where it has traditional reward systems.

Reward Systems—The Present State

Just what is wrong with traditional reward systems? Why are they not adequate to deal with today's demanding competitive environment? The reasons are several.

Rewards Are Not Tied to Organizational Performance

Traditionally, companies increase compensation year-in and year-out with little regard for the financial performance or the competitive position of the company. In truly difficult times, of course, a company may freeze wages and salaries temporarily or reduce the amount of the annual increase, but it is only a matter of time before compensation costs resume their relentless upward march. When this compensation increase is not accompanied by a concomitant increase in productivity, as was typical in the '70s and early '80s, the outcome is an increase in the unit cost of products or services. This is not a particular problem if competition is light; these cost increases are simply passed through to the customer.

In a highly competitive environment, on the other hand, this disconnect of compensation from the organization's performance soon lands the company in trouble. The unit cost increases cannot be readily passed through, and the company's profitability (or market share) declines. The loss of competitiveness may ultimately threaten the very survival of the business.

Wages and Salaries Are Inflexible

Below the executive level, compensation is essentially a fixed cost. Yes, management can reduce hourly compensation costs somewhat by cutting back on overtime, but if significant cost relief is required (as in a recession or a major competitive crisis), the only real option is to reduce the work force. Such action causes organizational turmoil, carries hidden costs, is detrimental to employee commitment and morale, and is incompatible with the principles of participative management.

Those organizations seeking to meet the competitive challenge through the creation of a high-commitment, high-involvement organization can no longer ignore the issue of employment security. It is simply unrealistic to expect that employees will feel a sense of partnership with management and ownership for the business when they suffer a loss of their livelihoods at every dip in the economy.

Organizations that rely exclusively on fixed pay, however, are severely limited in their ability to weather a business downturn without work force reductions. There is simply no other way to obtain significant labor cost relief.

There Is Little Reinforcement for Improving Performance

This is perhaps the most serious failing of traditional approaches to rewards. Rewards clearly influence behaviors, and if a company does not explicitly reward those behaviors that are critical to the organization's success, it should not be surprised if those behaviors fail to occur.

Executives today are quick to use the term "pay-for-performance" in describing their reward systems, but this is largely an exercise in self-delusion. Their "merit" increase systems are a sham, as true merit typically accounts for only a small portion (if any) of the employee's salary increase. The major influences on individual increases have nothing to do with merit, but reflect such things as cost of living changes, the individual's position in his salary range, budget constraints, and political considerations. In addition, the merit system is typically administered in such a way that the differential between high and low performers is miniscule. As a result, merit systems often turn out to be little more than cumbersome methods of administering across-the-board increases.

The non-reinforcing nature of reward systems is even more glaring at the hourly worker level, where pay increases are normally based on seniority, dictated by the union contract, or applied across-the-board. There is literally nothing in it for hourly employees to improve productivity and organizational performance.

In a competitive environment where constant improvement in quality and productivity is a prerequisite for success, businesses simply cannot afford non-reinforcing reward systems.

Dual Pay Systems Create a Two-Class Culture

The existence of two different pay systems, one for salaried employees and one for hourly employees, telegraphs management's cynicism about the worker. Salaried employees apparently are trustworthy, honorable, motivated, and loyal, so there is no need to monitor their working hours or to tie their compensation precisely to their hours worked.

The different treatment of the hourly worker, by contrast, would seem to be a manifestation of a different set of assumptions: these workers are lazy, unreliable, unmotivated, and untrustworthy. Management tracks their presence on the job to the minute and penalizes them for even minor tardiness. Corporations aggravate the situation by maintaining different benefit programs for salaried and hourly employees and top it all off by providing special perks and privileges to salaried people. Then they launch employee involvement or team-oriented programs. They tell their hourly employees that they trust them, value their input, and view them as partners in the business. Is it any wonder that corporations encounter skepticism and resistance to their entreaties?

Reward System Innovations

It has been observed that of all of the management processes, reward systems are the slowest to change. If this is true, it is not surprising because changes in reward systems directly impact the financial well-being of employees and can therefore be traumatic. This slowness to change is also unfortunate because reward practices probably have a greater impact on employees' behaviors than almost anything else that management does. And doggedly sticking with outmoded or ineffective reward systems in the face of a rapidly changing business environment is surely a recipe for failure.

The good news, however, is that reward system practices *are* changing now, perhaps at a greater rate than has been seen for decades. Non-traditional approaches to rewards, some of which represent rather dramatic departures from tradition, are spreading rapidly in American industry.

The all-salaried work force, for example, is helping to eliminate that two-class culture and thereby fostering collaboration toward common goals. Pay-for-knowledge, or skill-based pay, rewards the acquisition of additional skills by employees and serves as an enabling mechanism for team-based job design. Delivering merit increases in the form of lump-sum bonuses improves the reinforcing properties of the venerable merit increase and eliminates the annuity aspects of merit pay. Some further discussion of these approaches, all of which can co-exist with gain sharing, will be found in Chapter 13.

The focus of this book will be on a particular non-traditional reward system—gain sharing—that offers perhaps the greatest promise because it is one of the most universally applicable and addresses to some degree all of the reward system problems described earlier. Gain sharing is not new; its roots go back at least to 1935. What *is* new is its widespread use in American industry. The recent growth of gain sharing is driven by business conditions—intense competitive pressures and an emerging management philosophy that focuses on people. It can be a powerful tool to meet today's competitive challenges, and as such, it is a reward system whose time has come.

What Is Gain Sharing?

For our purposes, gain sharing will be defined as follows:

A compensation system that is designed to provide for variable compensation and to support an employee involvement process by rewarding the members of a group or organization for improvements in organizational performance. Gains, as measured by a predetermined formula, are shared with all eligible employees, typically through the payment of cash bonuses.

The above definition conveys several important implications that distinguish gain sharing from more traditional forms of reward:

◇ Gain sharing is a *group incentive*. Bonuses are based on the performance of an organizational entity, or sub-unit of that entity, and are distributed to all eligible members of the group in some equitable fashion. While a small number of plans do consider individual performance in distributing bonuses (Lincoln Electric being the notable example), this is not generally advisable. Gain sharing is designed to promote teamwork in improving performance, and any attempt to reward differential contributions on an individual basis can seriously undermine this objective. This does not mean that individual performance should no longer be rewarded; it does mean that other reward systems should be used to do it.

◇ Gain sharing is not a discretionary system, but rather requires a *pre-determined formula and payout mechanism*. If employees do not understand what is being measured or do not comprehend the basis for calculating bonuses, much of the power of gain sharing will be lost. In addition, it is an unfortunate fact of life that employee trust of management is low in many American organizations. And where low trust exists, a discretionary or ill-defined system will suffer from credibility problems and a suspicion on the part of employees that management will manipulate the system to suit their own needs.

◇ Gain sharing involves a *current payout*. This feature distinguishes gain sharing from traditional profit sharing plans in which the payout is deferred until retirement. While deferred profit sharing can perform a useful purpose (namely, providing employees with retirement income), it is questionable whether such plans, given their distant reward, can significantly increase employee involvement in improving performance. Profit sharing plans that pay cash bonuses, on the other hand, do meet our definition for gain sharing.

◇ Gain sharing is a *self-funding pay system*. Because bonuses are paid only when there are gains to be shared, this form of compensation increase should not adversely affect the company's costs. This characteristic differs markedly from more traditional approaches to pay, where increases may be influenced by changes in the cost of living, changes in area pay scales, union demands, and a variety of other factors. These increases may not be offset by performance improvement and thus result in increased costs and reduced competitiveness.

◇ Perhaps most importantly, gain sharing is a system that is philosophically consistent with the principles of *participative management*. Experience has shown that gain sharing is not very effective in a traditional, autocratic work culture. In such an environment, the employee has little opportunity to bring about improvements in organizational performance; his job is designed to minimize his discretion, and his supervisor is not particularly receptive to his ideas. Indeed, the only real opportunity to improve a gain sharing formula under these circumstances lies in working harder. Any other contributions, which could have far greater impact, are not possible. Organizations that are contemplating gain sharing, therefore, would be well advised to consider whether the culture and management practices are developed to the point where gain sharing can meet its full potential. Because of its importance, this issue will be developed further in the following chapter.

Why Gain Sharing Now?

The growth in the use of gain sharing in the United States has been rapid in recent years. A 1987 survey conducted by the American Productivity and Quality Center and the American Compensation Association indicated that 73% of the existing gain sharing programs at that time had been implemented within the previous five years. The survey further indicated that only 8% of the programs had been installed for more than ten years.[1] Obviously something has happened that has caused American businesses to become interested in gain sharing.

What has happened, of course, is the massive change in the business environment, and the associated need to modify reward systems to support the new business strategies. Gain sharing meets today's business needs in several ways.

First of all, by tying pay to organizational performance, gain sharing creates a layer of variable compensation. Compensation rises when organizational performance is high and declines when it is not.

Variable compensation offers several important benefits. Unlike traditional approaches to fixed compensation, the company increases pay (at least the variable portion of it) only when it can afford to. A company that is twice as productive as its competitors can (and should!) pay its employees twice as much as does its competition. On the other hand, during periods of deteriorating business performance, when the company can ill afford high compensation costs, variable pay comes to the rescue by providing needed cost reductions.

Variable compensation provides another, more subtle benefit: it increases employment security. With fixed compensation, management can obtain cost relief during tough times only by laying people off. This solution is not very palatable to a company that is seeking to increase the commitment and involvement of its work force. How, after all, can a company expect employees to feel like they are part of the team when management jettisons them at the first sign of trouble? The cost relief provided by variable compensation lessens the need to reduce the work force and therefore supports an employment stability strategy that in turn supports a participative management process.

Gain sharing also represents a solution to another reward system problem: the lack of reinforcement for improving organizational performance.

It is a well-established principle that positive reinforcement is a powerful tool for modifying behavior. Unfortunately, the business community has failed to use this tool with a large segment of its work force (given the sorry state of salaried merit increase programs, one could argue that businesses have failed to use the powers of positive reinforcement for virtually *all* of its work force). It is hard to imagine a company achieving the status of world-class competitor with employees who obtain no tangible benefit from improved business performance.

Gain sharing, of course, provides that missing reinforcement. With a gain sharing plan in place, the motivation to work hard and, more importantly, to work smart is likely to be considerably heightened.

The third reason that gain sharing is a logical response to today's business needs is that it supports a team-oriented, high-involvement culture.

It may be difficult to find a company today that is not pursuing employee involvement, participative management, quality of work life improvement, or the team concept. These are noble objectives and offer the potential for dramatic improvements in organizational performance and competitiveness. The problem is that these initiatives represent a change from traditional management philosophies. They are therefore not supported by traditional reward systems that were designed in a different era, under different business conditions, and under a different set of management assumptions.

It is certainly true that greater employee involvement can be achieved without changing the reward system. However, experience has shown that progress toward a high-involvement culture will ultimately be impeded without a supportive reward system. The intangible benefits of involvement—greater influence over one's life at work, the pride that accompanies contribution, and the social benefits of being a team member—will sustain an employee involvement effort up to a point. Sooner or later, however, these good feelings will become routine and the Hawthorne effect will wear off. Employees will notice that the financial benefits of their involvement are all accruing to the company and will begin to ask, "What's in this for me?" It is probably unrealistic to expect that employees will make ever-greater contributions indefinitely when the bounty of their efforts accrues solely to the company.

Gain sharing, of course, solves this problem nicely. The company and its employees are now partners in a win-win situation, and one more barrier to a high-involvement culture has been eliminated.

Current Gain Sharing Use

How widespread is the use of gain sharing today and what are the results? The first in-depth analysis of these questions can be found in the aforementioned survey on the use of non-traditional reward systems in the United States. While the data is now somewhat dated, its insights are valuable nonetheless.

The survey focused on large corporations, with the respondent companies accounting for a full 9% of the American work force. While only the data on gain sharing is of relevance to us here, the survey report contains valuable information on the use of a wide variety of non-traditional reward systems.

The survey indicated that 13% of the responding companies had a gain sharing program somewhere in their organization. In addition, another 14% indicated that they used small group incentives.[1] As a point of clarification, the survey authors defined gain sharing as a system that applies to an entire organizational unit, such as a plant. Small group incentives, on the other hand, were defined as systems that tie compensation to the performance of an organizational sub-unit, such as a department or team. For our purposes, both approaches could be construed as gain sharing because both meet the definition provided earlier. The total use of these two systems was something less than the combined 27%, as some responding companies used both approaches.

Gain sharing's penetration into industry today is undoubtedly greater, as the growth rate has, if anything, accelerated since the survey data was collected. An educated guess would be that 30-35% of the Fortune 500 companies now have at least one gain sharing program in place. In most cases (at least in larger companies), the use of gain sharing is still in the experimental or pilot stage, although a few, such as Motorola and Dana Corporation, are using gain sharing extensively throughout the business.

Thus far, gain sharing is more likely to be found in manufacturing rather than in service industries. The percentage of manufacturers using gain sharing was found in the survey to be 20% as compared to 8% for service organizations.[1] One should not infer from this statistic that gain sharing is better suited to manufacturing industries; as we shall see, gain sharing can be successfully installed in virtually any industry. The greater use to date in manufacturing is probably the result of the growth of international competition, which has thus far had a greater impact on manufacturing than on service organizations.

In part because of the lower base of installed plans, the future growth in gain sharing can be expected to be greatest in services. A survey question regarding the intentions of non-users of gain sharing was interpreted by the authors of the survey to indicate that the number of plans in place would increase over the next few years by 76% in manufacturing and by 168% in services.[1]

One of the more telling survey statistics related to the effectiveness of gain sharing in improving performance. Eighty-one percent of the respondents reported that gain sharing had a "positive" or "very positive" effect on organizational performance.[1]

In summary, the latest available survey data tell us that gain sharing is becoming fairly widespread in American industry, is growing rapidly in use, and has a high success rate.

Does this mean that every organization should adopt gain sharing immediately? The answer to that is no. Gain sharing is designed to support a high-involvement culture, which represents considerable change for most organizations. For those organizations that are not committed to change or have a low capacity to support change, gain sharing has a high probability of failing in the long run. Any organization considering gain sharing should therefore assess its readiness before proceeding (see Chapter 14). The next chapter will explore further the nature of the culture that is most conducive to gain sharing.

Preview of Coming Attractions

The first two chapters of this book provide overview material; this chapter has reviewed the definition and rationale for gain sharing, while Chapter 2 discusses the important issues of management philosophy and corporate culture as they relate to gain sharing.

The focus of Chapters 3 through 11 will be on gain sharing design issues. The intention here is to review the many design options and to acquaint the reader with the experiences of companies in a wide variety of industries. The theme of these chapters will be that there is great opportunity to create a gain sharing system that uniquely meets the needs of the business.

Chapter 12 discusses a range of other issues that typically arise when contemplating the feasibility of gain sharing. How for example, should the existence of a gain sharing program influence decisions to increase base pay? How does gain sharing fit with an individual incentive program? How is gain sharing dealt with in union contracts?

Chapter 13 provides a brief overview of other non-traditional reward systems that were mentioned in this chapter and that are also growing rapidly in use. Some or all of these other systems can easily complement a gain sharing system.

Chapter 14 provides a suggested six-step implementation strategy for those organizations considering gain sharing. Lastly, Chapter 15 summarizes the key issues examined in this book.

Summary

The changes in the business environment during the years leading up to the decade of the '90s have been truly extraordinary. The emergence of tough competitors around the world and the increasing demands of customers have vastly increased the performance requirements of American business.

To meet these requirements, American management has had to rethink its fundamental philosophies and assumptions. The outcome of this self-examination has been a recognition of the importance of the human resource and a commitment to the principles of participative management.

Unfortunately, traditional reward systems were designed in a different era and do not support today's business imperatives. Compensation is essentially fixed and is not tied to the performance of the organization. Dual pay systems create a two-class culture. And perhaps most importantly, there is little reinforcement for employee contributions to increased performance.

While several non-traditional pay systems are emerging to deal with these problems, gain sharing perhaps offers the greatest promise. Gain sharing rewards members of an organization, as a group, for their contributions to improved business results. It thus provides the needed reinforcement and fits perfectly with today's participative management philosophies.

Reference

1. O'Dell, Carla and McAdams, Jerry, *People, Performance, and Pay.* Houston, TX: American Productivity and Quality Center, 1987.

Chapter 2

The Gain Sharing Culture

A reward system (or any other management system, for that matter) should support and reinforce the management philosophy and organizational culture in which it is implemented. If a company were to install a reward system that is intended to promote a certain type of behavior, but that behavior was discouraged by other management practices and systems, the company would be working at cross-purposes. The result of such ambiguous signals from management would be skepticism regarding management's intentions, lack of employee enthusiasm for the new initiative, and ultimately an ineffective reward system.

Those outcomes are fairly predictable if gain sharing is implemented in a traditional organizational culture. What is a traditional culture? It is one in which few decisions are made at the working level, management systems focus on control, there is little information sharing, and employees have little opportunity to influence the course of events in their work area. Management systems and practices are clearly based on the assumption that employees have little to contribute to the success of the business. In this environment, gain sharing is out of place and will not likely meet expectations.

Fortunately, this traditional culture is gradually giving way to a new one that is almost certainly more effective in today's difficult competitive environment. John Sherwood, a consultant in organizational change, summed up the need to change when he said, "Today's competitive markets demand a high level of performance from everyone, not mere compliance to rules or obedience to supervisors."[1]

What Is Employee Involvement?

What Sherwood is referring to, of course, is an organizational culture that is characterized by high involvement and teamwork at all levels. Organizations of all kinds are pursuing this ideal; a study conducted by the U.S. General Accounting Office (GAO) in 1987 found that over 80% of the responding firms had some form of employee involvement activity under way. Yet many of these efforts have not lived up to expectations or have not stood the test of time. An analysis of the GAO data by the Center for Effective Organizations at the University of Southern California led to the conclusion that only 25% of the companies have made significant changes in the way most of their employees are managed.[2]

This finding is probably not surprising in view of the tendency of many companies to "plug in" employee involvement programs without considering the need to change other systems (selection, promotion, information sharing, job design, etc.) that are sending contrary signals. In this situation, powerful forces (in the form of traditional systems) will undermine the involvement effort.

Fortunately, companies are beginning to recognize that real cultural change can only occur when they rethink the basic management assumptions that underlie the systems and practices of the organization. It would be worthwhile to explore at this point how some of these assumptions are changing.

Role of Employees. Traditionally, management has viewed employees as extensions of machines. This assumption probably dates back to the early days of the Industrial Revolution, when employees in general had little education and enormous improvements in efficiency were to be had by replacing laborious manual processes with machinery. As the pace of technological change accelerated, greater and greater emphasis was placed on capital investment and technology as the keys to success. Technology was the Holy Grail. The potential contributions of employees to the success of the business were given little thought. People were simply necessary appendages; someone had to push the buttons and oil the gears. The technocrats in recent years have even gone so far as to dream of the "peopleless factory"; if we could just eliminate people from the production system, all of our problems would surely be solved.

General Motors, enamored of this vision and under pressure from tough Japanese competitors, embarked upon a $40 billion capital expenditures program in the mid-1980s. The intent of this ambitious undertaking was to enable GM to build cars that were competitive with anything the Japanese could produce.

What was the outcome? General Motors lost market share, not only to the Japanese, but also to Ford, which had focused on people-driven efforts to improve quality and reduce costs. Perhaps most galling of all, after all this money had been spent, the most productive assembly plant in GM's system turned out to be in Fremont, California; this plant was the least technologically advanced of them all.[3] Perhaps not so coincidentally, the Fremont plant is a joint venture with Toyota and is managed by the Japanese.

The savvy companies are rethinking their assumptions regarding the role of people. Rather than extensions of machines, they are beginning to view people as a resource that has not even begun to be tapped. It may just be that maximizing the contributions of people is at least as critical to competitive success, if not more so, as is technology.

Job Responsibility. The employee's responsibility has traditionally been to perform the task to which he has been assigned, and nothing more. Who determines *how* the task is to be performed? Certainly not the employee; that is the job of management or a technical specialist. Legions of industrial engineers have been turned loose in our nation's factories (and offices) to determine the one, most efficient method of performing the various tasks required to produce a product or service.

Once the task procedures have been defined (by someone who does not perform the task), it is then the supervisor's job to stand over the employee and ensure that he executes the task in the prescribed fashion.

Managers are coming to the realization that this assumption about job responsibility only serves to limit creativity, innovation, and performance improvement. The employee goes through the motions, doing his job in the way that he has been instructed. He has no latitude to do otherwise, and he is powerless to change the method of performing the task.

In today's highly competitive environment, more and more companies are attempting to redefine the employee's job responsibility from performing a task to continuously improving the performance of the system. This is not simply a minor shift in perspective; it carries enormous implications for culture change. For if employees are to continuously improve system performance, they must be provided with information, training, and power to a degree that was unheard of in the past.

Job Design. Much of our traditional thinking on job design can be attributed to Frederick Taylor, the Father of Scientific Management. Taylor's principles, developed in the early 1900s, focused on speciali-zation and maximum task breakdown. He taught that an organiza-tion's processes should be subdivided to the greatest degree possible, so that each worker's job was simple and repetitive. The employee would repeat his simple task hundreds, or even thousands, of times a day and would therefore become highly proficient at his job. Only through this approach to job design, the reasoning went, could the organization hope to achieve maximum efficiency in producing its product or service.

Taylor should not be criticized for his thinking; his principles were right for the time and served us well through much of the twentieth century. However, as world competition arose in the latter part of the century, some major weaknesses in the theory became apparent. When an individual's job is highly specialized, he has little sense of how his work fits in with the whole, and he does not feel that he is actually producing anything of value. IIe does not appreciate how his work affects other steps in the process, nor does he have reason to care. He has little sense of ownership for the finished product and little reason to take pride in his workmanship. His repetitive job is monotonous, tedious, and boring, and he therefore performs his job half-heartedly. And finally, with specialized tasks assigned to indi-viduals, management can expect little in the way of teamwork.

If managers want their employees to continuously improve the performance of the system, they must change their assumptions regarding job design. Workers must have a thorough knowledge of the whole process and how the various tasks interrelate. An employee in a world-class business will likely be multi-skilled and have broad responsibilities. He will probably be part of a team that produces an entire product or service and will have considerable input into how the productive process is executed. The multi-skilled, cross-trained work team consistently outperforms, in virtually every way, a collection of specialized individuals and is gradually becoming the norm in job design.

Information Sharing. The traditional attitude in American indus-try has been that information is to be provided to employees on a "need to know" basis. In other words, people are provided with only that information that is necessary to the execution of their narrowly defined job. This meant, of course, that employees were provided with very little information indeed.

This attitude conformed with the other traditional assumptions; if the employee's job was to perform a simple task precisely as instructed, what use would he have for any other information? Besides, communicating information broadly to the work force was time-consuming, expensive, and risky. After all, employees cannot be trusted to respect the confidentiality of business information.

If companies require maximum performance from every employee in order to be competitive, this assumption too much change. Their employees must understand both the nature of the business and how they fit into that business. They must know who the customer is and must fully understand his requirements. They must appreciate the competitive challenges facing the business. They must receive feedback regarding the performance of their work groups so they can solve problems and continuously improve. It is hard to imagine how people could perform at a high level without extensive information.

In addition, lack of information is a major cause of low trust in organizations. If employees do not understand the dynamics of the business and do not appreciate the rationale behind business decisions that affect their work area, they are invariably skeptical of management's intentions and have low commitment to the organization's mission. These characteristics are simply not conducive to the creation of a world-class competitor.

The assumption made by forward-thinking companies is that information sharing is critical to competitive success. Employees "need to know" virtually everything about the business.

Employee Input. In a traditionally managed organization, the employee has little, if any, input to decisions affecting his work area. His job is designed by management, and he is told what to do. His supervisor is not particularly receptive to his ideas, and process changes are made without consultation or explanation.

If he has any input at all, it is through traditional and structured vehicles such as attitude surveys and suggestion systems. While these can be useful mechanisms when properly supported by management, they allow for only periodic and limited input. The employee has little say about the day-to-day functioning of his work area.

A company can hardly expect to be a high-performing organization when the majority of its employees are not allowed to use their brains except under very limited circumstances. The organization is simply not using all of the resources at its disposal. Fortunately, this practice too is changing. Companies seeking to be leaders in their industry are providing for vastly increased input from their employees.

In fact, the degree of change has become extraordinary, as there are now numerous examples of self-managed teams. Also called autonomous work teams and self-directed teams, these small groups of employees effectively manage their own work area. They carry out virtually all of the functions formerly reserved for management, such as goal setting, scheduling, customer relations, problem solving, capital planning, discipline, hiring, and even firing. Unthinkable just twenty years ago, autonomous work teams now dot the industrial landscape. By any measure, this represents an extraordinary change in management thinking from the traditional mindset.

Means of Control. The traditional assumption is that employees must be tightly controlled. Hence many organizations have a proliferation of rules, regulations, policies, procedures, and standards. While policies and procedures may serve an important purpose in certain cases, such as in dealing with safety, legal, and environmental concerns, American management has unfortunately carried this felt need for control too far.

Multi-volume sets of procedure manuals, sometimes filling many shelves, rigidly prescribe the activities of people in every part of the organization. Supervisors, even middle managers, have little authority to make decisions or to deviate from established ways of doing things. Hundreds, even thousands, of people in many companies have nothing to do with supporting the production of a product or service, but are employed only to control others.

This control-oriented mentality effectively squelches the organization's ability to materially improve its performance or to adapt to change. There is only one right way to do things, and it doesn't matter that the procedure may have been written twenty years ago, when competitive conditions, customer demands, and virtually everything else were very different. Innovation and creativity are virtually nil. Change is discouraged, and deviation from the standard is punished. The status quo becomes entrenched and the organization calcifies. It cannot adapt to rapidly changing business conditions or competitive challenges.

Slowly but surely, controls are being loosened in American industry. The leading-edge companies are replacing rules, policies, and procedures with simple statements of management priorities, philosophies, and values. Employees at all levels are being given greater latitude in determining how things are to be done in their work area, consistent with the articulated management values.

If management says, "We exist to serve the customer, and the customer's satisfaction is the first priority," people will behave very differently than if they were told, "This is the procedure you must follow in doing your job, and don't deviate from it." Under the first scenario, the employee is focused on a key business priority and is empowered to do whatever is in the best interests of the company. In the latter case, the employee's hands are tied, and his focus is on covering his backside rather than on meeting the needs of the customer.

Company after company is loosening the reins of control so that employees at all levels can do what is necessary in pursuit of the real priorities of the business. Needless to say, this represents a radical departure from traditional practices.

Focus of Accountability. Traditionally, organizations and their systems have been designed around individuals. Jobs are designed for the individual, and it is a non-routine event for people to make team decisions. Performance-related rewards, if provided at all, are awarded to individuals. Employees know little about the functioning of the organization beyond their own work areas.

When people are treated as a collection of individuals, they naturally focus on their own jobs and have little regard for the impact of their work on other parts of the organization. They do not appreciate how they fit into the overall scheme of things, and there is little they can do to help their neighbor. Even if they could, they are not motivated to do so because that is beyond the scope of their job and will bring them no reward. It is unlikely in this individual-centered culture that people will work towards, or even share, common goals.

American business organizations are beginning to see that maximum organizational performance can only be achieved through a team-oriented environment. The team, not the individual, is rapidly emerging as the basic unit of organization.

These teams may or may not exercise a high degree of self-management. In any event, they are likely to be characterized by some degree of cross-training, job rotation, and team problem solving, with basic accountability for work vested in the team. Their base-pay system may well be a pay-for-skills system, in which a team member's pay is based on the number of jobs he is capable of performing, rather than on the task in which he is presently engaged (see Chapter 13 for a further discussion of this approach).

This change in assumption, of course, fits well with the others. If we want people to continually improve system performance and to work together toward common objectives, the team is the obvious vehicle to accomplish these ends.

Labor Relations. The traditional state of labor-management relations can be succinctly described in one word: adversarial. Labor and management, it was assumed, had different and incompatible objectives. One party, therefore, could only gain at the expense of the other. Anything that management wanted was automatically viewed by the union as detrimental to their interests, and vice versa. The obvious and unavoidable outcome of this assumption is that management and labor work at cross purposes in a win-lose proposition.

This assumption certainly must change if an enterprise hopes to survive the rigors of world competition. Tough competitors whose employees are working together with management toward common business objectives will surely prevail over any organization that is split into warring camps.

Formal labor-management cooperation efforts—hard to find in the 1960s, but common today—represent a manifestation of the growing acceptance by both parties of a different model. There are indeed many organizational issues outside of the collective bargaining process that are in both management's and labor's best interests to address in a collaborative, win-win fashion. Improvements in productivity, quality, customer service, quality of work life, safety, employee involvement, and a host of others serve both parties' interests by improving the competitive position of the business and making jobs more secure.

The Change Process

The idea that we need to change our basic management assumptions to meet today's competitive challenges is not new.

Richard Walton, in 1985, described "...two radically different strategies for managing a company's or a plant's work force, two incompatible views of what managers can reasonably expect of workers and of the kind of partnership they can share with them." The more traditional, control-oriented strategy, he notes, "simply cannot match the standards of excellence set by world-class competitors." The alternative approach is based on a belief that "...eliciting employee commitment will lead to enhanced performance." The choice of strategy, Walton notes, leads to considerably different decisions regarding such issues as job design, management style, degree of employee input, and labor-management relationships.[4]

Going back even further, Douglas McGregor's ground breaking work in the late 1950s gave us the famous "Theory X, Theory Y" dichotomy. Over 30 years later, McGregor's words are more meaningful than ever.

> If there is a single assumption which pervades conventional organizational theory it is that authority is the central, indispensable means of managerial control. Most of the other principles of organization, such as unity of command, staff and line, span of control, are directly derived from this one.
>
> In the management of the human resources of industry, the assumptions and theories about human nature at any given time limit innovation. Possibilities are not recognized, innovating efforts are not undertaken, until theoretical conceptions lay a groundwork for them. Assumptions like those of Theory X permit us to conceive of certain possible ways of organizing and directing human effort, **but not others.**
>
> Above all, the assumptions of Theory Y point up the fact that the limits on human collaboration in the organizational setting are not limits of human nature but of management's ingenuity in discovering how to realize the potential represented by its human resources.[5]

The purpose of the foregoing review of changes in basic management assumptions was to make a point. The competitive demands of today's global and fast-changing marketplaces have rendered our comfortable, tried-and-true ways of doing things obsolete; they simply won't suffice when the long-term survival of the organization is dependent upon obtaining the maximum contribution from all of the resources at its disposal. Managers simply cannot structure and manage their businesses in a way that minimizes the impact of people

Revamping our fundamental management systems is not a simple task, however. Present systems and practices, based on traditional assumptions, have existed for years, even decades. They are entrenched, and there are many people who have a vested interest in their continuation. Even those who recognize the need to change will have a difficult time in doing so, as their present behaviors have served them well, and have been repeatedly reinforced in the past. Under the best of circumstances, the transition to a different culture will be a long and arduous undertaking.

But the journey must be made. The 1990s is a very different world from that of the 1970s, and the organization that is mired in the ways of the past has about as much chance of survival as the dinosaur.

The essence of employee involvement or participative management is change. Those who view employee involvement as simply a quick-fix program to improve productivity or quality will fail. They will not address fundamental systems, practices, and assumptions that work against participation. Their efforts will be perfunctory, and all the forces that are dedicated to the status quo will undermine the effort. The program will be short-lived and soon forgotten.

The successful companies will undertake a process of change. There will be a commitment from the top of the organization to evaluate all existing systems for their conformity to the new set of assumptions and to change those that don't pass the test. There will be a dramatic increase in information sharing, so that employees will better understand the dynamics and priorities of the business. There will be a major commitment of resources to training, so that both managers and workers can acquire the skills needed to function effectively in a different culture. Particular attention will be paid to the first line supervisor, who is key to the change process but is often among the most resistant to change. And the leadership will understand that change does not occur overnight and will be prepared to stay the course.

There are now numerous examples of companies that have stepped up to this challenge of fundamental change in systems, practices, and culture. One of the longest-running efforts is that of Motorola, which established its Participative Management Program (PMP) in 1968. A 1981 company brochure describes PMP as "...a system of management—a culture if you will—that invites the participation and involvement of each of our employees in managing the affairs of our company." PMP is further characterized as:

◇ A structured, yet flexible way of managing the company on a continuing basis.

◇ A management system, not a plug-in program.

◇ Managerial encouragement and support of teamwork, idea sharing, and mutual trust.

◇ Increased two-way communication about the goals and objectives of the business, about how to achieve them, and about specific progress toward them.

◇ More decision making at the most appropriate level (which is usually lower in the organization).

◇ More employee responsibility where direction, discipline, and control are generally self-motivated and not externally imposed.

◇ A financial sharing of the benefits of improved productivity, quality, and service between the employees and the company.

Motorola must be doing something right; they were a winner of the Malcolm Baldrige National Quality Award in 1988.

Xerox (also a Baldrige award winner) is another company with a long-term management commitment to change. In the early 1980s, in response to the Japanese invasion of the plain-paper copier market, the company initiated a 15-year plan to transform the company's culture. As the company's internal literature put it, "Effectiveness through involvement is not a stopgap effort or a one-shot program. It is an ongoing process which is expected to grow—gradually but steadily—throughout the corporation until it is a way of life for all Xerox people."

Gain Sharing and Organizational Culture

How does all of the foregoing discussion relate to gain sharing? Ed Lawler, of the Center for Effective Organizations at the University of Southern California, states: "Unless most systems in an organization are changed to be congruent with participative management practices, ultimately participative management will not be effective."[6]

Traditional reward systems are simply not congruent with participative management. They do not reward involvement and they do not reward teamwork. If companies are to succeed in creating a new work culture, they need non-traditional rewards such as gain sharing. Without them, the reward system will become an ever bigger impediment to change.

Some managers make the mistake of assuming that a reward system like gain sharing will, by itself, motivate employees to achieve higher levels of performance. What they fail to appreciate is that a traditional culture throws up so many impediments to employees' improving performance that any motivational impact will largely be neutralized. Some of these impediments might be:

◇ Employees have little knowledge of the process beyond their narrowly defined jobs.

◇ Because little information is shared, employees do not comprehend the priorities of the business, the challenges posed by competitors, or the requirements of customers.

◇ Supervisors do not seek, and are not particularly receptive to, employee input.

◇ The emphasis on control ensures that any deviation from standard procedures in the pursuit of improvement is quickly squelched.

◇ The union, which views management as an adversary, resists any effort to directly engage the employee in problem solving. Management, at the same time, seeks to go around the union and worsens the already contentious relationship.

◇ Years of consistent signals from management that employees are of little value to the organization engenders employee skepticism and mistrust of management's motivations.

◇ Low job security, the result of countless layoffs, cost reduction programs, and restructurings, has ingrained the fear that any improvements in productivity will result in loss of jobs.

Is it realistic to expect that a new reward system, by itself, will overcome all of this? A research project by the University of Pennsylvania's Wharton School concluded:

> Managers of both successful and unsuccessful gain sharing programs consistently say that establishing a participative culture is the most critical factor for making gain sharing work. The successful programs incorporate the development of such a culture into every facet of the plan's operation and design.... The less successful ones were marked by internal contradictions in which the commitment to participation was undercut by actions that frequently discredited the program in the eyes of the employee.[7]

The conclusion that is inescapable is this: gain sharing, if it is to be effective, must be associated with an employee involvement process.

And an employee involvement process cannot succeed without management's commitment to change.

Make no mistake: *A company cannot buy employee involvement through gain sharing.* It can only obtain employee involvement through systems, processes, and practices that reinforce and institutionalize involvement as a way of doing business.

This leads to an obvious question: When is an organization ready for gain sharing? Must it have in place a high-involvement culture before it can expect gain sharing to work?

If the answer to the latter question was yes, there would be few gain sharing success stories, for few organizations can honestly claim to have achieved that high-involvement culture. In fact, it may well be impossible to realize the high-involvement paradigm without gain sharing; many companies have found that their involvement effort stalls at some point because of the lack of a congruent, reinforcing reward system. It is unrealistic to expect to establish a nontraditional work culture while retaining traditional reward systems.

The minimum requirements for gain sharing readiness are a management committed to change and some progress toward that desired future state of participative management. Progress means that the organization has increased its information sharing, has successfully implemented some basic involvement techniques, and has begun to address the impediments to change that are inherent in its traditional ways of doing things.

The organization that does not comprehend the need for change and has not yet begun the journey is not ready for gain sharing. For the organization that *is* committed to change, gain sharing can be a powerful tool to accelerate the process.

Summary

Efforts to transform the organizational culture to one characterized by highly committed, highly involved employees are widespread in industry today and are critical to the long-term survival of American industrial organizations. These efforts will succeed only if management rethinks its fundamental assumptions about people.

A company cannot expect its employees to continuously improve organizational performance when their jobs limit their latitude and ability to change the work process, when they are given little information about the business, and when all management systems focus on control. The company cannot expect to create a team-oriented environment when it manages people as a collection of individuals and maintains a win-lose relationship with unions.

These traditional beliefs and assumptions are ingrained in our work cultures and can only be overcome through a long-term and steadfast commitment to change. The change will be impeded, and may ultimately stall, if companies fail to provide reward systems that are congruent with the new set of assumptions.

Gain sharing supports a philosophy of participative management, and that should be its primary purpose. Where the commitment to change is lacking, the involvement process will be ineffective and gain sharing will fall short of expectations.

References

1. Sherwood, John J., "Creating Work Cultures With Competitive Advantage." *Organizational Dynamics,* Winter, 1988.
2. Lawler, Edward E., III, Ledford, Gerald E., Jr., Mohrman, Susan Albers, *Employee Involvement in America: A Study of Contemporary Practice.* Houston, TX: American Productivity and Quality Center, 1989.
3. "Shaking Up Detroit." *Business Week,* No. 3119, August 14, 1989, pp. 74–80.
4. Walton, Richard E., "From Control to Commitment in the Workplace." *Harvard Business Review,* March–April, 1985.
5. McGregor, Douglas, *The Human Side of Enterprise.* New York, NY: McGraw-Hill Book Company, 1960.
6. Lawler, Edward E., III, *High Involvement Management.* San Francisco, CA: Jossey-Boss Publishers, 1986.
7. Ost, Edward, "Gain Sharing's Potential." *Personnel Administrator,* July, 1989.

Chapter 3

Designing a Gain Sharing System

It would be unwise to design and install a gain sharing system of such importance without careful planning and preparation, including an objective assessment of the organization's readiness and capacity to support change. More than one gain sharing plan has failed because of inadequate planning and low organizational readiness. The important preparatory steps, as well as the design and implementation process itself, will be reviewed in detail later, in Chapter 14.

With readiness ascertained and preparation completed, the design process may begin. Management should be aware of several important considerations relative to the design of the gain sharing system.

The Design is Critical

The design of a gain sharing system is not a trivial matter. Gain sharing is a reward system, and it will have considerable impact on employee behavior. People will work to the measures, and, assuming the system is successful, management can expect an increase in compensation. It is therefore important that the formula be reflective of important business variables so that the additional compensation will be accompanied by financial gains for the company. Otherwise, the increased pay will not be properly funded and the system will be self-defeating. In addition, the system must be credible with employees and must pass the test of equity. It must also be flexible and adaptable to the vagaries of a dynamic business environment. A poor system design will (at best) render the program ineffective. At worst, it can set back the change process and have negative consequences on employee involvement, trust, and labor relations.

No "Best" Way

Any student of gain sharing will quickly discover several standardized plans (such as the Scanlon Plan) and many examples of customized systems used successfully by other organizations. There is a natural tendency to want to adopt one of these plans; after all, why reinvent the wheel? Managers seem to be particularly enamored of established models in their industry, as evidenced by the trend toward the use of similar systems among various companies in the electric utility industry, for one.

While it is undeniably useful (and important) to learn about the standardized plans and the experiences of other companies, it is a risky strategy to assume that what works magnificently in one organization may not be a dismal failure in another.

Organizations, even those providing similar products or services may be very different in terms of competitive position, culture, business strategy, labor-management relationships, pay levels, past history, education level of employees, management philosophy, maturity of involvement practices, and any number of other variables. All of these factors are potential considerations in designing a gain sharing system.

There are no rules in gain sharing system design, except those dictated by common sense and legal restrictions; therefore, an exceptional opportunity exists for a business to design a system that truly reflects its organizational characteristics and meets its needs. While a decision to adopt somebody else's plan will certainly shorten the design time, it may well result in a missed opportunity at best, and a failure at worst.

Complexity of Design

Several major design decisions must be made before a company can launch a functional gain sharing system. Generally several options must be considered for each of these decisions, and the choice can have significant implications for the credibility and effectiveness of the resulting system. In addition, none of these decisions can be made in a vacuum, for gain sharing is indeed a "system." All of the features must therefore fit together rationally and complement each other.

It is important to approach the design of a gain sharing system as a major undertaking; invariably, those charged with the design responsibility find that the difficulty and time requirements exceed their expectations. Resources must be provided and the time must be allocated to do the job right.

Design Components

A gain sharing system can be defined in terms of six major design components. At a minimum, decisions must be made relative to these six issues before a functioning gain sharing system is possible. In addition, there are several optional design components. A gain sharing system can exist and function without these features, but they may be important to the long-term viability of the system under certain circumstances.

There are many options for the various components, and no choice is right or wrong per se. Each of the options has certain advantages to recommend it; however, each has disadvantages as well. In essence, the design process involves thinking through the options, weighing the pros and cons, and selecting the one that best meets the needs of the business while ensuring that the system is rational as a whole and equitable to the employees.

The six required design components are summarized here.

The Group

Because gain sharing is a group reward system, one of the first questions a company must ask is, "Who's in the group?" This component is generally addressed first because many of the other design components cannot be intelligently resolved until a company has the answer to this question.

It would be difficult, for example, to make decisions about the gain sharing formula without knowing who is covered by the plan. The measures used should be meaningful to and, at least to some degree, controllable by the group. Other components, such as frequency of payout and bonus distribution, may be influenced by the group composition as well.

This component is sometimes disposed of rather quickly because management often has preconceived ideas about who should participate in gain sharing. It would be wise to think this issue through, however, because this decision will in some ways set the tone for the plan and will send an important message to the organization. In addition, certain options entail considerably greater risk than others and should not be selected without carefully weighing the risks against the benefits.

The options for this component are discussed in Chapter 4.

The Formula

The formula is the measure or measures that are used to quantify the organization's performance and therefore the gains to be shared. The formula is the heart of the system because it defines the kind of improvement that will be rewarded. It is probably the most important design component, and it is without doubt the most complicated one. Design teams may well spend more time on this component than on all of the others combined.

There is enormous flexibility and great opportunity for customization here. Many of the early gain sharing programs were designed to reward improvements in labor productivity or reductions in labor costs. There is no need (or even good reason) to limit the formula to such a narrow scope however; gain sharing programs today often address such variables as quality, material utilization, energy utilization, use of supplies, schedule compliance, service levels, safety, attendance, customer satisfaction, and employee involvement.

There are three major categories of formulas:

◊ Physical productivity measures, which reward improvements in the physical use of resources.
◊ Financial measures, which share with employees the gains associated with broader measures of business performance.
◊ Families of measures, which tie bonuses to a variety of specific performance indicators, often including non-cost variables such as quality, delivery performance, and safety.

The importance of the formula cannot be overstated, as it will have a major influence on the focus of employees' efforts and will be a direct determinant of the size of employee bonuses. The various formula options are reviewed in Chapters 5 through 8.

The Baseline

The size of a gain, or whether a gain is achieved at all, is determined by a baseline. The baseline is the value of the formula that must be exceeded in order to have realized a gain. The baseline is an important design issue because a given performance level can represent a large gain, a small gain, or no gain at all, depending on the baseline.

As with all the other design components, there is no "right" place to set the baseline. Many gain sharing plans establish the baseline at a level that corresponds to some previous level of performance, such as that achieved in the previous year. Other plans, however, will set the baseline equal to some target or standard that exceeds anything achieved in the past. This decision obviously has major implications for the credibility of the system.

A second major decision regarding this component is how often does the baseline change? The practical answers to this question range from never to frequently. This decision can be a difficult one and may also have a major impact on the employees' perception of the equity of the gain sharing system. These baseline issues will be discussed further in Chapter 9.

The Share

If gains are to be shared, managers must clearly establish how much will be retained by the company and how much will be paid to employees. They cannot simply say to their employees, "If we have gains, we'll share some of them with you." Such an ill-defined arrangement will surely harm the credibility of the program.

Many gain sharing systems use a 50/50 share, on the basis that an equal division of the gains between the company and its employees "sounds fair." While fairness is surely an important issue, and 50/50 would almost certainly strike the average employee as fair, it is not always the appropriate decision.

Perhaps more than any other design component, the share issue is dependent upon the outcome of other design decisions. It is influenced first of all by the choice of formula. It is also influenced by where the baseline is set and how the baseline changes. What is "fair" in one gain sharing system may not be fair in another.

One creative option is called a *variable share*. This feature ties the employee share to the level of another variable, such as profitability or quality. The share issues will be discussed in Chapter 10.

Payout Frequency

This component concerns the bonus payment interval. This interval can be as often as weekly or as infrequently as annually, with most programs falling somewhere in between.

While the motivational impact of this decision should clearly be considered, the more subtle implications for the viability of the gain sharing system should not be overlooked. The volatility of the formula also can be an important criterion in establishing the payout frequency.

Other creative possibilities such as *dual frequencies* and *variable frequencies* will be discussed in Chapter 10.

Employee Distribution (The Split)

The final required design component relates to the method of distribution of the employee share of the gains. This decision completes the loop by putting money in the employees' pockets.

This decision is far from trivial. There are three major options here, and the wrong choice can seriously undermine the perceived equity of the system. This component can easily become an emotional issue, and the debate on this decision can degenerate into a conflict between two camps, each attempting to pursue its own self-interest. This decision is further complicated by some legal requirements that limit the practicality of what is often the desired option. This component is explored further in Chapter 10.

Optional Design Components

The required design components are necessary elements of a gain sharing system—they cannot be ignored in the design process. However, there are a few additional components that are optional; a company may choose to incorporate them in the system design. These components are fairly common, and in certain situations, their use may be critical to the long-term viability of the gain sharing program. These components are summarized below and discussed in detail in Chapter 11.

Capital Investment Adjustments

A good argument could be made for excluding from the gain sharing system those gains that result from capital investments in new equipment and technology. These investments are made from shareholders' equity or with borrowed funds, and a certain return must be realized in order to justify the investment. If the capital-related gains are shared with employees, the necessary return may not be obtained.

At the same time, good arguments also exist for limiting these adjustments: employees do influence the success of a capital investment, and frequent adjustments to the gain sharing system may confuse employees and undermine the program's credibility. In addition, there are certain other design options—primarily associated with the baseline—that may obviate the need for these adjustments. If these adjustments are necessary, it is important to clearly define the nature and timing of these adjustments as an integral element of the gain sharing system.

Caps and Buy-backs

Another optional gain sharing component is a *cap*, or limit to the size of the bonus. Companies use caps for several reasons, which will be explained later.

Another optional feature often associated with a cap is the *buy-back*. A buy-back typically occurs when the cap is exceeded and the baseline is tightened in order to reduce the bonus payment to a level below the cap. To compensate employees for this change, a lump-sum payment is made to plan participants.

There are some good arguments for avoiding caps, and the need for them can be reduced through certain baseline options.

Smoothing Mechanisms

Formula volatility or seasonal variability can cause some undesirable outcomes from the company's point of view. At worst, they can result in employee bonus payments that exceed the total gain realized, a scenario that obviously would severely undermine the viability of the gain sharing plan. Accordingly, this issue is an important one and should not be overlooked.

The best-known technique for reducing the risk is the *deficit reserve*. Several other options exist, however, including the *rolling payout,* the *variable baseline,* and the *loss recovery*. As with other design issues, there are advantages and disadvantages with each of these options.

The Design Process

The design of a gain sharing program can, of course, be accomplished in several ways. Management can sit down and hammer out a system. Or a consultant can be called in to do the job on a turn-key basis. Probably the most effective approach, however, is to turn the job over to a team of employees. This team should represent a cross-section of the organization, including management members, union leaders, and rank-and-file employees.

The employee design team approach will probably take longer than the other options, because the team members will have to be educated in the dynamics of the business, and many diverse viewpoints on the design issues will have to be reconciled. The great benefit of this approach, however, is that employees will *own* the resulting system. There will be less need to sell the system to the participating employees, and few will question the equity of the program. Management will have to approve the system design, of course, and there is still a role for a consultant: that of facilitator, guide, and coach.

Further discussion of the make-up and role of an employee design team will be found in Chapter 14, Implementation Strategy.

Summary

An effective system design is a key success factor for gain sharing; the measures must reflect the priorities of the business, and the entire system must be equitable from an employee point of view. As a general rule, there are no right or wrong answers relative to the various design issues, and those involved should construct a system that fits the unique circumstances of the organization.

The design process basically involves the evaluation of alternatives associated with the six required design components. In addition, several optional components that serve important purposes should be carefully considered. The decision to design a gain sharing system should, of course, be deferred until the readiness of the organization has been assessed and the proper groundwork has been laid.

Chapter 4

The Group

The first major decision faced by those charged with designing a gain sharing system is *Who's in the group?* Because gain sharing is a group incentive, defining the boundaries of the participating group is of prime importance.

This decision must be made early because rational conclusions about many other design components cannot be reached without knowing who is participating in the plan. The formula must be relevant and meaningful to the participants and must measure things that they can improve. The payout frequency and distribution method will also more than likely depend on the choice of the group.

The group decision should not be taken lightly because it can have a major bearing on the success of the gain sharing program. There is no right or wrong choice, but rather several options (three basic ones, in this case) that are all potentially viable. The decision should be made by carefully weighing the advantages and disadvantages of the various options and considering how well each fits with the objectives of the program and the nature of the business.

Exempt/Non-exempt

Some companies choose to define the gain sharing group as a particular category of employees, such as the exempt or non-exempt work force (or alternatively, salaried or hourly employees). In the majority of cases where this course is chosen, the selected group is the hourly or non-exempt employees.

The reasoning for this decision often goes something like this: We presently have a reinforcing reward system for our salaried employees, and their performance is adequate. There is nothing, however, to motivate hourly employees to become more involved in performance improvement, as pay increases for that group are either contractual, general, or tied to seniority. Today's competitive circumstances require the greatest possible contribution from all of our employees, and we therefore must provide a performance-based pay system for our hourly work force.

The validity of this argument can be disputed. While salaried employees do typically have a merit increase system that is intended to reward performance, these systems are often administered in a woefully ineffective fashion (Chapter 13 describes a non-traditional approach to merit pay that can improve its effectiveness). And in many companies, the performance and teamwork of the white-collar work force wouldn't win any prizes. Nonetheless, it is probably true that generally a greater level of disaffection and less identification with business goals exists among the hourly work force.

As with any design option, potential drawbacks exist with the decision to select hourly or non-exempt employees only. Probably the primary concern is the effect on teamwork between the groups. The distinction between hourly and salaried employees often results in a "we/they" environment. The two groups are treated differently and see their objectives as conflicting. Many companies have concluded that this two-class system has a deleterious effect on business performance and are therefore striving to blur the line between the two groups (see the discussion of the all-salaried work force in Chapter 13). Under these circumstances, it may not make sense to create yet another system that treats one group differently than another.

The motivational effect on the group that is not included in the gain sharing program should also be considered. The hourly work force does not work in a vacuum. Salaried people certainly have significant impact on the performance of this group; the very reason for their existence is to support the operating activities of the organization. Will the support staff be as enthusiastic about their duties if the fruits of their labor are shared with others but not with them?

A final concern with this approach is the potential for pay compression. If the gain sharing program is successful, the total compensation of the hourly work force will rise relative to that of the salaried work force. This may exacerbate a problem that already exists in many organizations.

In spite of the various drawbacks, there have been some successful applications of this approach. One example is the Mobay Chemical plant in New Martinsville, West Virginia. Developed through a joint union-management effort in 1984, the Mobay plan shares with its more than 600 bargaining unit employees the gains associated with a variety of performance variables. Salaried employees are covered under a separate bonus plan.

Payouts in the Mobay plan are based on total cost savings, with a highly involving approach used to focus employees on improvement opportunities. Each department establishes a working group to develop departmental measures and goals for the upcoming year. These committees generally have four members, two hourly and two salaried. The plant's gain sharing brochure states that these groups should:

◇ Determine measurement areas.
◇ Publicize the program in their department.
◇ Monitor progress.
◇ Report monthly to the Productivity Fund Committee.
◇ Publish results for the department internally within the department.

Each departmental group determines areas to be measured such as yield, quality, maintenance, energy, and supplies, and sets targets for each in terms of cost savings. The total savings realized across the plant are shared, with all eligible employees receiving the same amount per hour.

In spite of the fact that only union employees participate in the plan, it appears to have been quite successful; management reports cumulative savings in excess of $5 million since the program's inception.

Site Inclusive

Probably a more common resolution of the group question today is to include all employees at a particular site in the gain sharing program. An obvious and common application of this approach is the use of gain sharing at a manufacturing plant. It can also be found at facilities that provide services, such as computer service operations, hospitals, and distribution centers.

We can even use the term *site* loosely to include broader organizational units, such as divisions or even entire companies. The "site inclusive" label will be used here in its broadest sense to describe any plan in which essentially all employees in a given organizational unit are gain sharing participants, covered by the same formula.

The phrase *essentially all* is used because even here there are often some minor exclusions. The usual exclusion is any employee who is presently covered by an executive bonus program. The reasoning is that the compensation of these senior managers is already highly tied to the performance of the organization, and presumably we want them to be more concerned with longer-term strategic business issues.

The other common exclusion is a sales force that is compensated on a commission basis. Here again, these people already have variable pay, and the nature of their work is often such that it makes more sense to provide sales people with an individual incentive rather than one based on group performance.

While the executive and sales exclusions are fairly typical, they are by no means mandatory. Plans that include both categories of employees do exist.

Some organizations exclude the "measurers"—those people who determine the quantitative values of the items being measured in the gain sharing plan. Who these people are depends, of course, on what is being measured; they might include accountants, industrial engineers, or quality control employees. If these people were included in the gain sharing program, the argument goes, the objectivity of their work could be compromised.

The "measurer" exclusion is not common, however, and rightfully so. These people are just as much a part of the team as everybody else, and their exclusion could simply create a new "we versus they" split in the organization. Besides, there are usually checks and balances to ensure that any fudging will not continue indefinitely.

The main advantage of the "site inclusive" option, of course, is that it helps promote the idea that all employees are part of a team working toward common objectives. There is no distinction between classifications or departments, and teamwork among line and support groups, across shifts, and between different levels now pays. In view of the problems that many organizations face with turf protection, finger pointing, and non-supportive support staff, this design option often makes eminent sense. In fact, it is probably the predominant choice in new gain sharing start-ups today. Well-known manufacturing companies with plant-level site-inclusive plans include 3M Company, Dana Corporation, General Electric, Pillsbury, Lennox Industries, Amoco Corporation, Mead Corporation, and Chrysler.

In the service industries, the site-inclusive approach has been adopted by Control Data, in their business services operation (see Chapter 8) and Sutter Health, in two hospitals in Sacramento.

The major potential drawback to the site-inclusive option is the potential inability of individual employees to closely relate to an organization-wide formula in a large operation. The employee may not understand the measure and may feel powerless to influence a formula that quantifies the performance of thousands of employees. Profit-sharing plans covering an entire corporation may particularly suffer from this shortcoming. Can a corporation really expect an employee to be highly motivated to improve something that he does not understand when he is one of 10,000 or more employees?

The problem is not limited to company profit-sharing plans, of course. Plants of 5,000 and more employees are not uncommon in industries such as automobiles and aerospace, and any plant-wide formula in these operations must, almost by necessity, be complex. In these situations, it may be useful to consider a third option for the group decision.

Functional/Product/Process Groups

The major objective for this option is to break the organization down into multiple groups, each with its own formula. In this approach, each employee's bonus is based on the performance of his subgroup rather than on the performance of the entire organization.

The primary attraction of this option, of course, is that the individual employee will likely relate better to the formula because it is measuring only the performance of his work area. And, as a member of a relatively small group, he probably will feel that his actions have a greater impact on the variables being measured. The result should be greater enthusiasm for the plan and heightened motivation to improve performance.

While these benefits are indeed enticing, this approach carries with it some sizeable risks. The first of these is the potential for *sub-optimization.* If the performance of the overall organization is dependent upon the different subgroups working together, it may be dangerous to focus each group's attention on the performance of its own work area exclusively. Under these circumstances, the group's increased enthusiasm for performance improvement might be accompanied by a corresponding decline in its concern for the impact of its actions on others in the organization. Optimizing the performance of sub-units in an interdependent organization may well lead to sub-optimum performance for the larger entity.

A second major risk associated with the multiple-group option is the potential for inequities, perceived or real. If one group consistently earns large bonuses, while another group consistently earns little or nothing, inevitably the latter group will find fault with the system. They will surely contend that the high-earning group had an easier formula. Worse yet, they may conclude that their inability to earn bonuses was due to the fact that they were already performing at near-maximum efficiency when the gain sharing program was installed. Their more fortunate colleagues, on the other hand, had a great deal of room to improve. The gain sharing program, therefore, simply rewarded those who were previously low performers while penalizing the real contributors. Whether these assertions have any basis in fact, the perception will obviously be detrimental to morale and to commitment to the improvement process.

There are also some administrative complications here. Keeping track of multiple formulas and multiple payouts may not be a simple matter. In addition, there is the problem of job transfers; how should an employee who spent part of the gain sharing period in a high-earning department and then transferred to a low-earning department be treated? To complicate matters further, what happens when an employee in a low-earning department is loaned temporarily to a high-earning department?

In spite of the pitfalls associated with the multiple-group approach, some organizations have made it work. One well-known success story is that of Nucor Corporation, a steel manufacturer based in Charlotte, North Carolina.[1] Approximately 3,000 direct production employees at various Nucor plants are covered by gain sharing. In addition, there are separate systems covering indirect employees, department managers, and senior executives.

The production workers are typically subdivided into groups of 25 to 30 employees for gain sharing purposes. The members of each shift and production line earn bonuses based on the productivity of their group. The measures are simple—generally units of product produced per hour of operation. The base against which improvement is measured was set several years ago, and there has been dramatic productivity improvement over time. As a result, it is not unusual for Nucor production employees to earn bonuses in excess of 100% of base pay. During a ten-year period beginning in the seventies, sales at Nucor rose 850%, while the number of employees increased by only 240%.

It should be noted that Nucor is an unusual organization, and its experience may be difficult to duplicate. The company is very entrepreneurial, with risk-taking and constructive conflict strongly encouraged. The company's human resource philosophy emphasizes mutual respect, trust, and fairness. Information is shared openly, and a formal procedure exists for any employee to question any management decision. All employees from top to bottom enjoy the same benefits, and there are no executive perks. It is also a very flat organization, with only five levels in the entire company.

The risks associated with the multiple-group structure can be ameliorated somewhat through a dual-level bonus system. Under this concept, employees would receive only a portion of their bonuses from their work-group formula, with the balance coming from an overall site-inclusive measure. This approach should lessen the suboptimization problem, as actions that negatively influenced other groups would also lessen a major part of the offending employee's bonuses. The consequences of perceived inequities among groups probably would be moderated as well.

A plant in LTV's Missiles and Electronics Group has taken this idea a step further by designing a gain sharing program with *three* payout levels. The plant in question, located in Camden, Arkansas, is divided into fifteen units, representing different stages of the manufacturing process. Employees who are assigned to one of these units receive a bonus based on the productivity of their unit as compared to forecasted efficiency levels.

This particular plant consists physically of two separate buildings. The unit employees also share in improvements in costs that are only measured at the building level or are difficult to attribute to a specific unit; these include support personnel assigned to the building; scrap (which, while identified at the unit level, may have been caused by an "upstream" unit), utilities, and rework. The sum of the unit efficiencies is also included in the building-level formula. Support labor, who are assigned to the building rather than to a specific unit, receive a double share of the building gains because they do not share in unit-level improvements.

Finally, there is an overall site gain sharing pool, which consists of the sum of the building-level improvements and selected overhead costs, such as office labor costs, travel expenses, office supplies, and telephone expense. Office employees receive their bonuses entirely from this source, with building and site employees receiving 50% and 25% shares, respectively.

The major drawback of this program, of course, is its complexity. Fortunately, LTV had the foresight to recognize that employee understanding of the program was important to success, and a significant resource commitment was made to an education and communications effort. This commitment has paid off, as bonuses approached $3,000 per employee by the second year of the program.

Summary

To summarize, the three basic options for the group component are:

◇ Exempt or non-exempt only.
◇ Site inclusive.
◇ Multiple groups, either with or without an inclusive measure overlayed.

The major concern about the first option is that by dividing the organization into two groups, it may be incompatible with the team philosophy. The site-inclusive choice is more common today, although large organizations may wish to consider the use of multiple formulas to enhance employee identification with the system.

The decision is an important one because it influences the complexity of the system design, the degree to which employees can relate to the gain sharing program, and the degree of teamwork that is promoted. It will almost certainly send a message to the organization, intended or otherwise.

Reference

1. "Case Study 28: Nucor Corporation." Houston, TX: American Productivity and Quality Center, 1983.

Chapter 5

The Formula

If companies are to share with employees the gains associated with improvements in organizational performance, they clearly must have a way of measuring that improvement. The *formula* is the means to accomplish this end. It is the measure (or measures) through which shared performance improvements are quantified.

The formula is clearly the heart of a gain sharing system, for it defines the type of improvement required to earn bonuses and, as a result, focuses employee attention on the variables involved.

While there are several viable options for each of the design components, the formula component is unique in that it offers almost limitless flexibility. The formula can be structured to reward improvements in virtually anything that is important to the success of the business from productivity, to quality, to customer satisfaction; even employee involvement itself is measured and rewarded in some systems.

The organization should not miss the opportunity to tailor the formula to its specific business needs; there is no need to force-fit somebody else's gain sharing formula. This chapter and the three following will review many actual formulas representing a wide variety of approaches.

The Formula Categories

Because there is such a wide variety of gain sharing formulas, it is useful to organize them into categories with similar characteristics.

The three major formula categories are:

◊ Physical productivity formulas
◊ Financial formulas
◊ Families of measures

Each of these categories is quite distinct from the other two and easily recognized when encountered. Each has quite different effects on employee behavior, and each represents different management philosophies about compensating employees.

Physical Productivity Formulas

Most textbooks define productivity in terms of a simple ratio:

$$\frac{\text{Output}}{\text{Input}}$$

It is a measure of the effectiveness with which the organization uses its resources in producing its output. Improving productivity simply means getting more out for what is put in.

While productivity has traditionally been associated with labor (particularly direct labor), the concept in fact is far broader. The organization in a competitive business environment must be concerned with using all types of input—materials, capital, and energy, as well as labor.

Physical variables, such as units per employee hour, units per machine hour, pounds out versus pounds in, and the like, should be used to accurately quantify productivity. Problems occur when companies attempt to measure productivity with variables denominated in dollars, such as revenues, payroll, costs, etc. Dollar-based ratios are influenced by changes in unit prices and unit costs as well as by changes in productivity. They mix apples and oranges and are therefore not pure productivity measures. A company cannot ascertain whether it used its resources effectively unless it measures productivity in physical units (or approximations thereof obtained by removing the inflation effect from dollar-denominated measures). The distinguishing features of the *physical productivity* category of gain sharing formulas is that the *use* of resources is being measured and it is being quantified in physical terms.

The primary attraction of physical productivity measures is that they represent performance variables that are largely under the control of the organization and its employees. They are not affected (at least not directly) by market conditions and other events that are external to the organization. How an organization uses its resources in producing products or services is up to the organization.

Proponents of physical productivity formulas argue that employees should be rewarded for improving those things over which they have direct control. If more units of product or service are produced without proportional increases in labor, capital, materials, or energy, then employees have done all that could reasonably have been expected of them, and the organization is better off as a result. A gain sharing system that failed to pay bonuses under these circumstances, they would argue, would almost certainly be rejected by employees as either flawed or inequitable.

The foregoing is certainly a compelling argument. What could be more reasonable than rewarding employees for factors that are under their control? This argument can be termed the *Controllability Philosophy*. A prerequisite of a physical productivity formula, of course, is that productivity be reasonably susceptible to quantification; this requirement may present some serious problems in certain types of organizations, primarily professional and technical ones. How does one measure physical productivity, for example, in an R&D organization? Apart from the measurement difficulties, we need to ask ourselves whether productivity (in a traditional sense) is even high on the list of important performance issues for that type of organization.

Productivity measures commonly exist, on the other hand, in most manufacturing facilities and in many service organizations that deliver discrete, quantifiable units of service. These measures typically have received a good deal of visibility, and employees may understand and be comfortable with them.

Some actual physical productivity formulas will be reviewed in Chapter 6.

Financial Formulas

While tying gain sharing bonuses to variables that employees control would seem to be an obvious decision, there is a potential problem in so doing: it is entirely possible that management could be increasing compensation when the profitability of the business is declining, or even negative. A company could have the most productive employees in the industry, but if its raw material costs increase dramatically or intense competition forces it to lower the price of its product or service, it may well face financial difficulties nonetheless. Paying high bonuses under these circumstances would be inconsistent with the variable compensation objective—paying employees more when business performance justifies it, and obtaining cost relief when times are tough. It could even be financially imprudent.

A second type of gain sharing measure is the *financial formula*. Basically, any measure that is denominated in dollars rather than in physical units qualifies as a financial formula.

A company might, for example, use a simple dollar-based measure of labor performance:

$$\frac{\text{Sales value of production}}{\text{Payroll costs}}$$

This is essentially the formula used in the famous Scanlon Plan (see Chapter 7). This formula still focuses on labor, but by quantifying the output in dollars, the formula introduces the effect of selling price, which is largely market-driven. The likelihood of paying large bonuses in periods of low profitability is certainly less than it would be under a physical productivity formula.

This idea can be taken a step further and an even broader measure applied:

$$\frac{\text{Sales value of production}}{\text{Controllable costs}}$$

The formula is now expanded beyond labor costs to include a wide variety of inputs. Because costs are measured in dollars, the formula introduces even more market-related factors—the purchase prices of various inputs. This formula now further reduces the risk of paying bonuses when the company's financial condition does not warrant doing so.

Apart from the benefit of tying bonuses more closely to financial performance, some analysts argue for financial formulas based on more philosophical principles. They contend that financial formulas represent an opportunity to increase employee awareness of, and commitment to, the business as an enterprise. With pay tied more closely to the performance of the business, employees will feel more like business partners with management and will recognize that their own well-being is inextricably tied to the success of the business. Everybody—employees, management, and stockholders—is in the same boat and will sink or swim together. This argument can be called the *Common Fate Philosophy*.[1]

The use of a financial formula increases the requirements for employee education and information sharing. If a company plans to obtain employee buy-in to a system that ties pay to overall business performance, it had better be sure that employees understand the business and the external forces that impact financial performance. And when these external forces cause bonuses to decline, the company must ensure that employees appreciate the reasons their efforts have not been translated into higher pay.

Clearly, management must ask itself some fundamental questions before it can make an intelligent decision on the formula. Does it want to reward employees for improvements that are under their direct control, or does it want to tie compensation to broader measures of business performance? Physical and financial formulas are very different animals, and they can produce dramatically different outcomes in terms of employee behaviors and pay. It is entirely possible to have a blend of the two approaches.

Later chapters will discuss techniques to introduce an element of Common Fate into an otherwise Controllability-oriented plan. Financial formulas will be discussed in more detail in Chapter 7.

Families of Measures

The third general formula category is of more recent vintage than the other two, and is growing more rapidly in use. The principal attraction of the *family of measures* is a high degree of flexibility and a greater potential for customization.

A family of measures formula is characterized by multiple measures, each independent of the others. Each of the measures contributes to (or detracts from) the overall bonus payout. The individual elements of a family of measures can be either physical or financial, although in practice they tend to be controllable in nature.

The family of measures approach provides a logical answer to potential weaknesses of the other two formula categories. While a physical productivity measure is highly controllable, it is at the same time a narrow measure; it does not reward employees for a variety of other performance variables over which they have some influence and control. A financial measure, on the other hand, can be quite broad in its coverage but may hinder employees from relating their efforts in improving productivity, materials utilization, and so on, directly to the formula. In addition, financial formulas are offensive to those who espouse the Controllability Philosophy.

With a family of measures, a company can build a gain sharing program around specific, highly controllable indicators of employee performance in a variety of key areas. In addition, the family of measures enables management to explicitly reward improvements in non-cost variables, such as safety, schedule performance, and customer satisfaction. These potentially critical factors are normally not explicit in either a physical productivity or financial formula.

The family of measures is also more flexible in terms of adapting to changing business conditions. As circumstances warrant, individual indicators can be dropped and new ones can be added relatively simply.

These advantages do not come without a price; developing a family of measures formula is considerably more complicated and time-consuming than are the other two formula categories. By comparison, physical and financial formulas are fairly straightforward, and there are only a limited number of measurement options to choose from. Designing a family of measures, on the other hand, may entail sorting through and analyzing dozens of potential indicators to find the ones that are most appropriate for gain sharing.

The family of measures, including specific examples, will be discussed in greater depth in Chapter 8.

Summary

The formula is the heart of a gain sharing system, as it identifies the types of improvements that will be rewarded and quantifies the gains to be shared. This design component offers the organization the greatest opportunity for customization to the characteristics and needs of the business.

All gain sharing formulas fall into one of three categories. Physical productivity formulas measure the internal use of inputs in producing outputs of goods and services. Financial formulas are denominated in dollars and are thus affected more directly by marketplace conditions. The family of measures approach uses multiple indicators to quantify gains; as such, it is a broader formula than one based solely on physical productivity, yet can be constructed to minimize the uncontrollable aspects that are typical of financial formulas.

Reference

1. Credit belongs to Carla O'Dell of O'Dell & Associates for developing the "Controllability" vs "Common Fate" nomenclature.

Chapter 6

Productivity Formulas

Physical productivity formulas measure the use of resources in producing goods or services. Because both input and output are measured in physical units (or approximations thereof), the influence of external events—increased competition, changes in purchase costs, etc.—is minimal. Changes in the level of these measures are largely controlled by the organization's employees. Physical measures are therefore manifestations of the Controllability Philosophy.

While the vast majority of physical productivity formulas are designed to measure labor productivity alone, this category should also include any system that measures, in physical terms, the use of raw materials, energy, or any other input. However, if multiple measures are used, the formula becomes, by definition, a family of measures.

We will first look at a popular standardized approach to measuring physical productivity, and then examine some customized systems.

IMPROSHARE®

Developed by industrial engineer Mitchell Fein in the mid 1970s, IMPROSHARE® is an example of a standard plan to measure physical productivity.[1] A standard plan is a predetermined system design that is used in many companies. While there may be some tailoring to meet the unique circumstances of each organization, the basic structure is recognizable from one installation to the next.

The principle advantage of a standard plan is that someone has already figured out the formula, and it has a track record of successful use. While this can be comforting, management should take care to ensure that the standardized formula fits the business needs, data systems, and compensation philosophy of the organization. A homegrown system often justifies the extra time commitment and allows for greater employee involvement in the system design.

IMPROSHARE® (an acronym for Improved Productivity through Sharing) uses direct labor standards to measure the aggregate productivity of all of the organization's employees. A hypothetical example of an IMPROSHARE® formula is presented in Table 6-1.

Table 6–1
Example of IMPROSHARE® Formula

Basic Data

Units of Production:
   Product A – 400
   Product B – 600
   Product C – 300
Standard Direct Labor Hours/Unit:
   Product A – 5
   Product B – 3
   Product C – 2
Base Productivity Factor – 2.15

Formula Calculation

A: 400 units × 5 hours × 2.15	4,300
B: 600 units × 3 hours × 2.15	3,870
C: 300 units × 2 hours × 2.15	1,290
IMPROSHARE® Hours	9,460
Actual Hours	8,790
Gain	670
Employee Share (50%)	335
Actual Hours	8,790
Bonus Percentage	3.8%

The first step in the calculation is to multiply the units of production for the period (units of service could be used as easily as units of product) by the appropriate direct labor standard, in hours. Standards, which are estimates of the amount of time required to produce one unit of product, are generally only available and meaningful for direct labor (those employees that actually manufacture a product or deliver a service). Hours of indirect labor—maintenance workers, accountants, engineers, supervisors—are not directly attributable to producing units of product.

Indirect labor is not left out of the picture, however. It is taken into account by the *base productivity factor,* which is the value of the following ratio during the base period (typically the year preceding the launch of the gain sharing plan):

$$\frac{\text{Total Hours Worked}}{\text{Standard Direct Labor Hours Earned}}$$

The numerator includes the hours of all participating employees (including salaried people). The denominator, a common measure of output in manufacturing firms, is obtained by multiplying the units produced during the base period by their respective direct labor standards.

This base productivity factor (2.15 in the example) thus serves to quantify the total hours that would have been required in the base period to produce the output in question. As Mitch Fein puts it, "The BPF represents the relationship in the base period between the actual hours worked by all employees in the plant and the value of the work in hours produced by those employees, as determined by the measurement standards used in the base period. In effect the BPF is a means to "use up" all hours worked and to factor into the original standards all occurrences which were not included in the standards."[1]

The base productivity factor, then, accomplishes two important purposes:

◇ It provides for the inclusion of employee hours for indirect and salaried employees whose time is normally not covered by standards.
◇ It establishes base period efficiency as the baseline against which improvement will be measured. In other words, employees earn bonuses not by beating the standard, which may lack credibility with them, but by improving over the base period performance level.

After completing the calculations (units produced × direct labor standard × base productivity factor) for each product or service line, the resulting numbers are added to obtain IMPROSHARE® hours. Conceptually, this figure represents the total hours that would have been expended at base-period efficiency levels to produce the output in question. The actual hours for the period can then be subtracted, and the result is the number of hours saved through greater productivity. These savings could come about through increased output, reduced hours (either hourly or salaried), or both.

In the final step, the employee share of the gain, which is 50% in IMPROSHARE®, is divided by the total hours worked to obtain a percentage bonus for the period, which is typically a week.

In IMPROSHARE®, the standards and base productivity factor are frozen. While most companies would change their labor standards from year to year to reflect current efficiency levels, the standards used for this gain sharing program remain fixed at base period levels.

Does this mean that an organization that succeeds in realizing continuous improvement must pay higher and higher bonuses *ad infinitum?* The answer is no because of another feature of IMPRO-SHARE®: there is a 30% cap on the bonus payout.

A cap, of course, introduces a new problem: how does an organization continue to motivate people to improve productivity once the cap has been exceeded? IMPROSHARE® solves this problem through the use of a deferral account and a buy-back of the standards. These features will be discussed in Chapter 11.

As Table 6-1 shows, there are no dollar signs in this entire calculation. The formula measures physical productivity, pure and simple. By using standards in calculating output, a built-in weighting system exists; changes in product mix (and even the addition of new products) are handled effectively without distorting the measure.

Table 6-2 presents a partial list of companies that have used IMPROSHARE®. While predominately used in manufacturing, the plan has been adapted to service industries, including a bank, an airline, and a hospital.

Table 6-2
Companies Using IMPROSHARE®

Bell & Howell	Ingersoll-Rand
Carrier Corporation	Johnson & Johnson
Champion Spark Plug	John F. Kennedy Medical Center
Columbus Auto Parts	McGraw Edison
Adolph Coors Company	Phillips Petroleum Company
Eaton Corporation	Pitney-Bowes
El Al Israel Airlines	Prestolite
Firestone Tire Company	Rockwell International
General Electric Company	Security Pacific National Bank
Hooker Chemical Company	TRW
Huffy Corporation	

Source: Mitchell Fein, Inc.

The 3M Company

The 3M Company, the widely respected manufacturer of adhesives and a host of other products, developed their own physical productivity gain sharing formula in the early 1980s. Initially installed on an experimental basis in five plants in 1983, the system can now be found in over 15 locations.

Like IMPROSHARE®, the 3M plan uses direct labor hours (based on either a standard or historical data) to measure a plant's output. The mechanism used is different however, and is called an *equivalency factor*. The first step in calculating the equivalency factor is the selection of one of the plant's products as the base product. This is an arbitrary decision, and the choice has no impact on the resulting system; it serves simply as a base against which to calculate the relative labor intensity of the various products. The direct labor standard for each product is then divided by the standard for the base product to obtain the equivalency factors. An example of this calculation is shown in Table 6-3.

Table 6–3

3M Equivalency
Factor Calculation

Product	Direct Labor	Equivalency Factor
X20	2.0 Hrs.	1.0
L100	16.2	8.1
B150	12.4	6.2

To quantify the plant's output for a given period, the units of production for each product are multiplied by the appropriate equivalency factor to obtain equivalent units. This calculation is shown in Table 6-4.

Why not simply use actual units produced rather than go through the additional step of calculating equivalent units? The purpose, of course, is to provide a weighting system to ensure that changes in product mix do not distort the productivity measure; an organization can clearly produce more of a low labor content product than it can of a high labor content product with a given number of hours worked. It should be noted that IMPROSHARE® accomplishes the same thing by multiplying each product's unit production by the standard itself.

Table 6–4

3M Output Calculation

Product	Equivalency Factor	Units Produced	Equivalent Units
X20	1.0	20	20
L100	8.1	100	810
B150	6.2	200	1240
		Total	2070

Having quantified the output, 3M now can measure productivity by dividing the equivalent units by the total hours worked in the facility, as such:

$$\frac{\text{Equivalent units}}{\text{Hours worked}}$$

This ratio, calculated quarterly, is then compared with its average value for the previous 12 quarters (see Chapter 9 for further discussion of the "rolling baseline" concept) to determine a percentage improvement. This percentage gain is divided by two to determine the employees' bonuses expressed as a percent of pay.

The 3M plan has an additional feature that is worthy of note: a *quality penalty*. Any defective product that is returned from the customer and scrapped by the company results in a triple deduction from the current period's output. For products that are returned for repair or rework, the hours associated with the rework are tripled and added to the "hours worked" (the denominator of the ratio). The message is clear: productivity improvement will be rewarded, but not at the expense of quality.

For those 3M plants that regularly subcontract work, there is an additional adjustment made to the productivity ratio. In effect, the hours that would have been expended had the work been done internally are added to the denominator. If this adjustment were not made, the productivity ratio could be improved by contracting work out, that is, more final output could be obtained without an increase in hours worked.

The full gain sharing ratio, then, looks like this:

$$\frac{\text{Equivalent units – quality penalty}}{\text{Hours worked + subcontractor adjustment + rework penalty}}$$

The value of this ratio is compared to the average of the previous 12 quarters to determine the gain to be shared.

The 3M plan has been very successful at some locations; one plant reported a 65% improvement in productivity, along with a significant reduction in the cost of quality, over a four-year period.

The 3M approach and IMPROSHARE® have some similarities: both are built around measures of physical productivity, both use direct labor standards as a weighting mechanism, and both plans include virtually all employees.

The differences may be more important than the similarities, however. 3M pays bonuses quarterly, while IMPROSHARE® is a weekly-payout plan. IMPROSHARE® uses a fixed baseline, while the 3M baseline changes quarterly. IMPROSHARE® has cap and buy-back provisions; 3M does not. And the 3M plan has an explicit and powerful quality penalty, while IMPROSHARE® does not (although only good products are counted in IMPROSHARE®).

St. Luke's Hospital

A good example of a physical-productivity plan in a service industry that is quite different from the previous examples is the one in place at St. Luke's Hospital.

St. Luke's Hospital is a 686-bed, not-for-profit institution in Kansas City, Missouri. Concerned about rising health-care costs and the associated pressures from insurers, St. Luke's began experimenting with a gain sharing program in 1979. While the program initially applied to only six departments, it was gradually expanded until it was implemented throughout the organization in 1985.[2]

The St. Luke's plan is an example of the small-group gain sharing approach—gains are calculated at the department level based on a simple formula: controllable costs per unit of service.

Using this formula throughout the organization requires, of course, that each department (there are about 85 of them) define a unit of output or service. For some departments, this was a relatively simple task; the output of the pathology lab, for example, is the number of tests run. For others, it required some imagination.

But how can a cost measure be categorized as a physical productivity formula? Isn't the St. Luke's plan based on a financial formula? While the St. Luke's formula does measure costs in dollars, it nonetheless is equivalent to a physical productivity measure because the costs are *deflated;* that is, the effects of price changes are removed.

Any changes in the measure from year to year, therefore, reflect differences in *the use* of resources. That is productivity, and it is highly controllable.

St. Luke's also differs from the other productivity gain sharing systems profiled in this chapter in that it includes more than just labor input. In common usage, the term "productivity" is often interpreted to mean labor efficiency. This is an unfortunate and limiting perspective, as an organization must be concerned with the effective use of all of its resources if it is to succeed in a demanding competitive or economic environment.

To ascertain whether a gain has occurred in a particular department at St. Luke's, the cost measure is compared to its average value for the preceding two years (like the 3M plan's rolling baseline). Bonuses are paid annually based on the full year's performance.

The St. Luke's plan has another important feature: bonuses are paid only if the hospital achieves its financial objectives for the year. This provision ensures that the institution will not incur further financial losses in a bad year by paying bonuses to those departments that do manage to improve productivity. To be completely accurate then, we must really categorize the St. Luke's plan as a hybrid; to qualify for bonuses, employees must improve measures of physical productivity. But the payment of those bonuses is contingent upon overall financial performance.

During the first few years of the St. Luke's plan, bonuses were paid only to those departments that improved their departmental productivity measures. This proved to be a problem, as the laggard departments often contended that their failure to improve productivity was due to the actions of other departments or outside forces. As a result, the plan was modified so that all departments received a bonus when the hospital exceeded its financial objectives, with a larger share going to those departments that succeeded in improving their productivity measure.

The willingness of St. Luke's to modify a plan that was flawed reinforces an important gain sharing principle: the organization must have the flexibility to change a gain sharing system over time to correct problems or to adapt to changing business circumstances. This point will be discussed further in Chapter 14.

The St. Luke's plan appears to have been successful by almost any standard; the hospital reports multi-million-dollar savings in each of several years during the 1980s.

Summary

The primary attraction of physical productivity formulas is that they are not heavily influenced (at least not directly) by external events. As such, they can be useful indicators of the real contributions made by the organization's employees. They are reflective of the Controllability Philosophy—the belief that variable pay should be tied to factors that are under employee control.

The strength of controllability-oriented measures might also be viewed as their weakness, for they may yield significant bonuses during times of poor financial performance due to uncontrollable economic or marketplace conditions. In addition, they limit the use of gain sharing to issues of resource utilization, thus inhibiting the use of this tool to reinforce such important variables as quality, service levels, delivery performance, and safety.

The other two formula categories address some of these issues but, as we shall see, also have some problems of their own.

References

1. Fein, Mitchell, *IMPROSHARE®; An Alternative to Traditional Managing.* Hillsdale, NJ: Mitchell Fein, Inc., 1981.
2. "St. Luke's Hospital: Gain Sharing in a Not-for-Profit Environment," *The Productivity Letter.* Houston, TX: The American Productivity and Quality Center, January, 1987.

Chapter 7

Financial Formulas

Financial measures are those that are denominated in dollars rather than in physical terms. This is not a minor difference, for dollar-denominated measures are much more likely to be affected by external events such as changing marketplace and competitive conditions. If, for example, output is defined as sales (or sales value or production) changes in selling price could be expected to have a significant impact on this measure. Because selling prices in most industries are largely market-determined, a major uncontrollable factor is introduced into the equation.

By the same token, if inputs (labor, raw materials, etc.) are monitored in dollar terms rather than in physical units, another largely uncontrollable element—the purchase price of these inputs—must be considered.

Whether this is good or bad depends on a company's compensation philosophy and the objectives of the gain sharing program. Financial formulas would have no appeal to those who believe that bonuses should be tied only to factors that are under the employees' control. They are perfect, on the other hand, for those who espouse the "Common Fate Philosophy." Common Fate proponents argue that bonuses should be tied more closely to the success of the business, for that is the ultimate determinant of the organization's ability to pay higher compensation.

Financial formulas require a greater commitment from management to share information and to provide economic education to the work force. For obvious reasons, it is important that employees understand the external forces that may reduce or eliminate their bonuses in spite of their best efforts. Lacking this knowledge, they will likely blame their misfortune on management decisions or, worse yet, management manipulation of the numbers.

One could argue, of course, that management should long ago have educated their employees in the dynamics of the business anyway.

How can the work force be expected to be committed when employees lack even a basic understanding of the enterprise and the factors affecting business performance?

Financial formulas, then, are quite a different animal from their physical cousins. As such, they produce different results, have different advantages, and carry different risks. We will first examine the standard plans in this category, and then we will look at some customized approaches. We will also take a quick pass at the ultimate financial formula, profit sharing.

Standard Plans

As is the case with physical productivity formulas, there are certain standardized plans that have been widely used over the years. These include the Scanlon Plan, the Rucker Plan®, and the Multi-Cost Ratio, which is really a modified version of the Scanlon Plan.

The Scanlon Plan

Probably the best known of the gain sharing plans, the Scanlon Plan is also considered the oldest, with its roots dating back to 1935.

It was in that year that Joseph Scanlon, the president of a local of the United Steelworkers Union, approached the president of Empire Steel and Tinplate Company, located in Mansfield, Ohio. Scanlon had an idea that he thought might save Empire, which was in danger of failing in the Great Depression.

Scanlon's idea, which was somewhat radical at the time, was to engage the company's employees in efforts to improve productivity and cut costs. Empire's president decided to give it a shot, and Scanlon organized a series of departmental committees, each consisting of some hourly employees and their supervisor. Employees were encouraged to submit their ideas to their departmental committee, which had the sanction to evaluate and implement these ideas within certain bounds. A plant-wide steering committee was also formed to evaluate wide-ranging, complex, or costly ideas. Hourly employees also served on this steering committee along with members of management.

The initiative was a smashing success and was even credited with helping Empire survive the depression. Word spread, and soon Scanlon was performing his magic in other companies. He even became associated with Douglas McGregor, of "Theory X/Theory Y" fame.

McGregor felt Scanlon's system was an excellent vehicle for Theory Y companies, discussing it at length in his ground-breaking work on the subject.[1]

The early Scanlon Plans did not have bonuses associated with them; they were simply an employee involvement technique. It wasn't until the 1940s that the bonus feature was appended to the program. It has been an integral element of the process ever since.

Basically, the traditional Scanlon Plan formula relates labor costs to sales value of production (a service organization could, of course, simply relate labor costs to sales or to value of services delivered.) A typical Scanlon formula is presented in Table 7-1.

Table 7-1
Scanlon Plan Formula

Sales	$2,000,000
Less Returns, Discounts, Allowances	50,000
Net Sales	1,950,000
Plus/Minus Change in Inventory	250,000
Sales Value of Production	2,200,000
Allowed Labor Costs (20%)	440,000
Actual Labor Costs	400,000
Bonus Pool	40,000
Less Company Share (25%)	10,000
Employee Share	30,000
Less Contribution to Deficit Reserve (25%)	7,500
Amount to be Distributed	22,500
Participating Payroll Costs	$350,000
Bonus Percentage	6.4%

The starting point for the Scanlon formula is sales, from which customer returns and any discounts or allowances are deducted in order to arrive at net sales.

If the program is to be installed in a manufacturing facility, it is generally desirable to relate labor costs to production levels, as manufacturing costs are driven by production rather than by sales. In order to derive a value for production, any increase in inventory should be added to net sales and any decrease in inventory should be subtracted. The resulting figure represents the value of production at selling prices. It should be noted that the inventory adjustment should include changes in finished goods and possibly work-in-process, but not in raw materials.

After establishing the output for the period, a targeted labor cost, called Allowed Labor, can be derived. This is done by applying a percentage to the sales value of production. This percentage is historical in nature, representing the average ratio of labor costs to production value during a prior period, typically one to three years. This figure would normally include benefits as well.

To determine the gain, if any, the actual labor and benefit costs for the period are subtracted from that allowed. A positive number indicates that less labor cost was incurred, as a percentage of production value, than in the base period.

The company then subtracts from the bonus pool its share of the gain —traditionally 25%. The remainder represents the employee share.

There remains another step before the employee share can be distributed, however. A portion of the employee share—typically 25%—is deducted and set aside in a reserve account, called the deficit reserve. The purpose of the deficit reserve is to enable the company to recover a portion of earlier (or later) gains in the event of a deficit period—one in which labor costs exceed the allowed labor ratio. As one of several mechanisms to reduce the risk associated with variability in the formula, the deficit reserve will be discussed in greater detail in Chapter 11.

The amount that remains after the contribution to the deficit reserve is then distributed to eligible employees as a percent of their total pay for the period. The percentage is determined by dividing the amount to be distributed by the participating payroll. Note that the participating payroll is less than the actual labor costs used earlier in the calculation, as the latter includes benefit costs.

The Scanlon Plan pays bonuses monthly. The allowed labor ratio may not change over time, or it may be reviewed and reset annually to allow for an equal bonus-earning opportunity each year.

There are a number of variations on the Scanlon formula; one example is the "split ratio" formula, in which gains are calculated separately by product line. Each line has its own allowed labor ratio, reflecting differing labor intensities. The various gains are added together to determine the bonus pool, which is then distributed in the normal fashion. The advantage of the split ratio is that changes in product mix are accommodated without distorting the gain sharing results.

As is true of all dollar-based formulas, the Scanlon Plan is suscept-ible to influences from outside forces, primarily those that drive changes in the selling price of the organization's products or services. Because production is valued at selling price, with allowed labor costs a predetermined percentage of this value, any increase in selling price will, other things being equal, increase the bonus pool. This is a two-way street, of course, and any price reductions (or increase in dis-counts) will likewise reduce employees' bonuses. This element of un-controllability, of course, is not repugnant to Common Fate proponents.

Any student of gain sharing will quickly discover that virtually all the examples of long-lived gain sharing programs are Scanlon Plans. One should not assume from this phenomenon that Scanlon Plans are the only ones that stand the test of time; rather, it is simply a manifestation of the fact that Scanlon was the major form of gain sharing existing prior to the 1970s.

The continuing existence of these long-running programs is evi-dence that gain sharing can become institutionalized as an integral element of an organization's culture. Examples of Scanlon Plans with over 30 years of history include Herman Miller, Inc., the manu-facturer of office furnishings located in Michigan, and Atwood Indus-tries, an automotive equipment supplier in Rockford, Illinois.

The Rucker Plan®

Another standardized gain sharing plan using a financial formula is the Rucker Plan®, developed in the late 1930s by Alan Rucker, an economist. Rucker modified Scanlon's idea in a way that at first appears to represent a rather insignificant variation, but in fact changes the focus of the gain sharing program considerably. Rucker's idea was to express labor costs as a percentage of *value added* rather than as a percentage of sales value of production.

Value added is a quantification of the additional market value created when a manufacturer transforms raw materials into finished product. It is calculated by subtracting from the sales value of produc-tion the costs of all purchased inputs—raw materials, energy, sup-plies, etc. How does this transformation take place? It happens through the application of labor and capital equipment. In essence, the company purchases materials and then uses labor and capital to transform these materials into something different—something that has greater value in the marketplace than did the original inputs. The measurement of value added is conceptually simple; the value of the purchased inputs are subtracted from the value of the output (sales value of production).

An example of a Rucker® calculation is presented in Table 7-2. As in the Scanlon Plan, it arrives at sales value of production by subtracting the various deductions from sales and adjusting for changes in inventory. However, it deviates from the Scanlon model by subtracting from production value all purchased materials and services and yields value added.

Table 7–2

Rucker Plan® Formula

Sales		$1,500,000
Less Returns, Discounts, & Allowances		50,000
Net Sales		1,450,000
Plus/Minus Change in Inventory		(30,000)
Sales Value of Production		1,420,000
Less Outside Purchases:		
Raw Materials	640,000	
Energy	110,000	
Supplies & Purchased Services	90,000	840,000
Value Added		580,000
Allowed Labor Costs (42.3%)		245,340
Actual Labor Costs		225,600
Gain		19,260
Less Contribution to Deficit Reserve (20%)		3,852
Amount to be Distributed		15,408
Participating Payroll		184,000
Bonus Percentage		8.4%

Then the allowed labor ratio is applied which, like the Scanlon approach, is based on historical experience. The difference is that the allowed labor ratio is applied to value added rather than to production value. Actual labor costs are subtracted from allowed labor to quantify the gain. After deducting the contribution to the deficit reserve, the remainder is divided into participating payroll costs to obtain the bonus percentage.

At first glance, the Rucker® formula may appear to be simply a different way of calculating and sharing improvements in labor costs. A closer analysis, however, reveals that the Rucker Plan® is quite different from the Scanlon Plan.

Note that an increase in value added will generate a bonus with this formula. A reduction in material losses, for example, reduces the amount of materials that must be purchased for a given level of production. This increases value added, which in turn increases allowed labor costs, as they are simply a percentage of value added. Assuming actual labor costs do not increase, the savings in materials is shared. The same would apply to savings resulting from lower use of energy, supplies, or any other purchased input.

Note also that the Rucker Plan® bonus is influenced as well by changes in the *costs* of purchased inputs. Any increase in the price of raw materials or energy will, other things being equal, reduce the value added and hence the bonus. This does not hold true if these cost increases are passed on to the customer in the form of higher selling prices; there is no effect on value added in this case.

It is now apparent why the Rucker Plan® is much broader in scope than the Scanlon Plan. Employees are rewarded for improvements in the use of a wide range of inputs and are influenced by changes in the costs of the inputs as well. It is the strongest "Common Fate" orientation of any plan reviewed to this point.

A plan that incorporated elements other than labor in its formula was an important development in the history of gain sharing. Employees certainly have the capability of improving the use of most inputs, and if it makes sense to reward them for higher labor productivity, why not also reward them for improving the productivity of other factors as well? More recent approaches to gain sharing even include many non-cost variables such as meeting delivery schedules and improving safety.

The Rucker Plan® has one significant peculiarity. As Table 7-2 shows, the total calculated gain goes to the employees. Does this mean that there is no benefit to the company?

For any increase in value added, there actually is a company share—it is the complement of the allowed labor ratio. For each dollar increase in value added, allowed labor in our example would increase by 42.3¢. The remainder of the enhanced value added (57.7¢) is retained by the company. You will recall from our earlier discussion that value added is increased through the application of labor and capital to the purchased inputs. In essence, the employee share of the gain is equal to the traditional contribution of labor to value added. The company keeps the contribution attributable to capital.

But the company-share question is not yet fully answered. Rucker Plan® participants have another avenue, besides increasing value added, to earn bonuses—they can reduce labor costs. A quick look at the formula example reveals an interesting phenomenon—employees receive a 100% share of labor cost reductions! For this reason, some companies have deviated from the traditional Rucker Plan® calculation by subtracting a company share from the gain. This of course considerably reduces the true employee share of value-added improvements.

In spite of the obvious benefits of a broader formula, examples of the use of the Rucker Plan® are harder to find than the Scanlon Plan and its variants. This probably stems from the fact that the Rucker Plan® is somewhat complicated and probably difficult for the average employee to understand. A simpler, and more popular, way to incorporate inputs other than labor is a variation of the Scanlon Plan called the Multi-Cost Ratio, which will be reviewed in the next section.

Multi-Cost Ratio

While the Multi-Cost Ratio may simply be viewed as a variation of the Scanlon Plan, it is nonetheless a major approach that needs to be discussed in its own right. It considerably broadens the original Scanlon idea, and it is probably more common today than the traditional version of the Scanlon Plan.

An example of a Multi-Cost Ratio is presented in Table 7-3. It differs from the Scanlon Plan in a single, but significant way: it includes additional costs beyond labor.

It is a flexible system; it may include only two or three major costs, such as labor, materials, and energy, or it may include all of the operating costs of the business.

Whatever costs are included are handled just as they are in the traditional Scanlon Plan. An allowed ratio is developed based on the historical relationship of these costs to sales value of production (or sales in a service business); actual costs are deducted from the allowed value; and the remainder is shared between the company and its employees. Unlike the labor-only Scanlon Plan, the employee share

Table 7-3
Multi-Cost Ratio

Sales		$3,460,000
Less Returns, Discounts, Allowances		54,000
Net Sales		3,406,000
Plus/Minus Change in Inventory		328,000
Sales Value of Production		3,734,000
Allowed Costs (81%)		3,024,540
Actual Costs		
Labor	$589,070	
Materials	1,540,840	
Energy	314,390	
All Other	519,740	2,965,040
Bonus Pool		59,500
Less Company Share (65%)		38,675
Employee Share		20,825
Less Contribution to Deficit Reserve (20%)		4,165
Amount to be Distributed		16,660
Participating Payroll		532,490
Bonus Percentage		3.1%

of the gain is not likely to be as high as 75%, for reasons that will be discussed in Chapter 10.

The Multi-Cost Ratio has become popular in American industry because it is a simple, straightforward way to motivate and reward employees for improving a wide variety of costs. There is no reason to limit gain sharing to labor costs only, particularly when there may exist even greater leverage in reducing losses on raw materials or other inputs. The Multi-Cost Ratio is a system that provides flexibility to the gain sharing company; it may include as few or as many cost items as the company deems appropriate.

An example illustrating the potential of the Multi-Cost Ratio can be found at the Custom Plywood Division of Eggers Industries.[2] Located in Two Rivers, Wisconsin, the company in the early 1980s was seeking an alternative to an outdated individual incentive plan. With the cooperation and consent of its union, the United Brotherhood of Carpenters and Joiners, the company organized a joint labor-management task force to explore employee involvement and gain sharing. The outcome of this effort was a formal employee involvement program, supported by gain sharing in the form of a Multi-Cost Ratio.

After evaluating the various costs of the business, the task force concluded that employees had at least some influence on 36 separate items of cost. When aggregated, these costs amounted to 81.5% of sales value of production. Improvements in this ratio were shared, with 55% of the gains going to the workers.

By the fourth year of the program, the ratio had declined to 69.6% of sales, a dramatic improvement by almost any standard. Bonuses in that year amounted to almost $3,300 per employee.

The key factor here is that the Eggers gain sharing program was more than just a reward system; it was an element of a participative management process. The driver for improvement was employee involvement, and the company and the union had the foresight to recognize the role of a non-traditional reward system in supporting that process.

The principal drawback to the Multi-Cost Ratio is that it, like the Rucker Plan®, is also influenced directly by changes in selling prices and the purchase costs of the items included in the formula. The best efforts of employees to improve the use of resources can be wiped out by an increase in the cost of materials, supplies, or energy. While Common Fate advocates would not object to this feature, many companies are not comfortable with subjecting employees' pay to the risks of the marketplace.

For those who wish to eliminate the price impact, there are two basic alternatives.

◊ Include production and/or the various cost elements at some frozen or standard cost. This avenue, of course, detracts from the simplicity of the formula. Some examples will be reviewed later in this chapter.
◊ Forget the Multi-Cost Ratio and develop separate measures of the *use* of each of the key inputs. This option is the Family of Measures, which will be discussed in the next chapter.

Profit Sharing

Any book on gain sharing would be incomplete without a discussion of profit sharing. Profit sharing, of course, is the ultimate Common Fate formula, as bonuses are based on the bottom-line performance of the business.

Profit sharing meets our definition of gain sharing only if bonuses are paid in cash. The more traditional form of profit sharing, involving a deferred payout, represents a fine retirement program but arguably does little to motivate involvement in performance improvement activities. In addition, deferred profit sharing programs are rarely linked to employee involvement change efforts. Cash profit sharing, on the other hand, could in theory support an involvement process.

The principal attractions of profit sharing are that it ties pay to overall business performance (eliminating the risk of paying bonuses when the business is faring poorly) and promotes identity with and commitment to the company's business goals. It is also relatively simple to design, therefore reducing considerably the time and resource commitment required to launch the system.

At the same time, profit sharing suffers from some rather severe drawbacks. Employees do not normally understand how profits are derived, and profit sharing has the least "line-of-sight" of all the approaches to gain sharing; it may not be apparent to plan participants how their actions translate into higher pay. Profit sharing also has a high element of uncontrollability (from the point of view of the average employee) because it is heavily influenced by a variety of external events, senior management decisions, and arcane accounting practices.

In a large company, profit sharing is probably more effective when it is based on the profitability of an operating unit (division, plant) rather than on that of the company as a whole. This at least brings it closer to home for the employees involved.

Ford Motor Company

Ford's plan is an example of cash profit sharing at its simplest. Originally negotiated with the United Auto Workers union in 1982, the plan has paid substantial sums (in excess of $3,000 each in some years) to the company's employees.

The bonus pool is a percentage of fully accounted after-tax profits. The percentage specified in the 1982 contract was a sliding scale, as follows:

◇ 10% of profits exceeding 2.3% of sales
◇ 12.5% of profits exceeding 4.6% of sales
◇ 15% of profits exceeding 6.9% of sales

Bonuses are paid annually in cash and distributed based on a percentage of the employee's pay for the year. An interesting feature of the plan is that the employee may elect to take all or a part of his bonus in the form of a contribution to the company's 401(K) plan.

The Ford plan probably stemmed as much from labor negotiation imperatives as from a desire to support an employee involvement process. The plan's effect on individual motivation to improve performance is dubious in a company with several hundred thousand employees. But it does illustrate a straightforward approach to the mechanics of profit sharing and has undoubtedly served a useful purpose for the company and its employees.

Motorola

Motorola, the large electronics company, has developed an interesting variant of profit sharing that increases employees' ability to relate the bonus more closely to their efforts.

Motorola has been relentlessly pursuing change through their Participative Management Program (PMP). Dating to the late 60s, the objective of PMP has been to create a high-involvement, team-oriented culture throughout the company. An integral element of this process has been gain sharing.

For many years, Motorola used the small group approach to gain sharing; teams of 25-50 employees earned bonuses based on the performance of their teams in improving such things as quality, costs, delivery performance, and safety in manufacturing. Support functions, such as engineering and finance, had a separate plan tied to the achievement of their operating unit's profit plan and to goals that were specific to their functions.

In part because of equity concerns (see discussion on multiple groups in Chapter 4), Motorola in 1988 implemented a completely different plan—one in which bonuses for both manufacturing and support employees would be tied to the profitability of Motorola's six business sectors.

For each sector, the bonus pool is a function of return on net assets, or RONA. Below 8% RONA there is no bonus pool. As RONA increases from that threshold, the bonus pool, as a percent of payroll, increases proportionally until it reaches a maximum of 15% of payroll.

While Motorola dictates that all sectors use the formula in determining the size of their bonus pool, they have left the distribution of that pool to the discretion of sector management. Each sector can therefore develop performance criteria that are specific to the sector and more meaningful to employees. Motorola thus has profit sharing with a twist: the size of the bonus pool is a direct function of profitability, but how and to whom the pool is distributed is determined by more meaningful and controllable performance measures.

A particularly interesting example of sector performance measures are those selected by the Government Electronics Group (GEG), located in Scottsdale, Arizona.

At GEG, all employees are on teams, and any employee qualifies for a share in the sector bonus pool as long as his team meets three requirements:

◇ It has three or more *goals* set by the team and approved by a steering committee. Note that the goals only must exist and be published; they do not have to be met in order for team members to earn a share of the pool.
◇ It must have an established *communication system*, designed by the team, to ensure timely dissemination of information to team members.
◇ It must have *problem-solving* teams to identify and solve workplace problems.

In essence, Motorola's Government Electronics Group has chosen to make profit-sharing bonuses contingent upon active participation in the Participative Management Program rather than on performance improvement in a traditional sense. This organization obviously is committed to the employee involvement process and has demonstrated it by tying profit-sharing bonuses to employee involvement per se.

There are two conclusions to be drawn here. One, profit sharing can be made more meaningful and effective by making payouts contingent upon achieving gains in variables over which employees have greater control. The second is that gain sharing can be tied to anything that is deemed to be important to the success of the business. Measures need not be limited to labor productivity or performance. If it makes business sense to do so, measures of employee participation or anything else that is deemed to be a priority can be used.

Sealed Power Technologies

Another illustration of how profit sharing can be made more meaningful to employees is provided by the Contech Division of Sealed Power Technologies. Headquartered in Kalamazoo, Michigan, Contech is a supplier of components to the automobile industry.

In the Contech program, which covers five plants, the bonus potential is determined by division *operating profit compared to plan*. The chart in Table 7-4 indicates the potential bonus available, as a percent of employees' pay, based on various levels of plan performance. No bonus can be paid if operating profits fall below 85% of plan, while the maximum potential bonus is 8%.

Table 7–4
Sealed Power Technologies Bonus Potential

Division Operating Profit as % of Plan	Potential Bonus
115 or greater	8.00%
112.5–114.99	7.75%
110–112.49	7.50%
107.5–109.99	7.25%
105–107.49	7.00%
102.5–104.99	6.75%
100–102.49	6.50%
97.5–99.99	6.00%
95–97.49	5.50%
92.5–94.99	5.00%
90–92.49	4.00%
87.5–89.99	3.00%
85–87.49	2.00%
Less than 85	0.00%

One-half of the potential bonus is paid to all participating employees at all plants. The remaining half is contingent upon the achievement of goals established for each plant in six performance areas:

◇ Productivity
◇ Rework
◇ Customer rejects
◇ Scrap
◇ Safety
◇ Attendance

Each goal carries a weight, with the total of the weights equaling 100. These weights determine the percentage of the remaining half of the potential bonus that is attributable to each goal. A goal with a weight of 20, for example, would earn 20% of the plant-performance half of the potential bonus.

Each plant determines the weights to be applied to each of the goals, and the goals themselves are established by an employee committee at each location. Thus the goals are plant-specific and are established in a fashion that is congruent with the philosophy of employee participation.

The Contech plan is classified as profit sharing because potential bonuses are a direct function of profitability. But the use of plant-specific goals considerably enhances the relevance of the program for employees.

Customized Plans

Most customized financial plans are variants of the Multi-Cost Ratio or profit sharing. Here are some examples.

Dresser-Rand

A joint venture between Dresser Industries and Ingersoll-Rand, the Dresser-Rand plant in Painted Post, New York manufactures air compressors. Their gain sharing formula is presented in Table 7-5.

Dresser-Rand positioned gain sharing as part of its employee involvement process. An employee brochure on the gain sharing program outlines the details of the formula only after several pages of discussion on the involvement effort.

The Dresser-Rand plan is a minor variation of the Multi-Cost Ratio approach; it uses three separate ratios in order to better highlight the major improvement areas: labor costs, quality (as measured by spoil-

Table 7–5
Dresser-Rand
Gain Sharing Formula

Net Sales	$9,000,000
Inventory Change	1,000,000
Sales Value of Production	10,000,000
Target Labor & Fringe (16.23%)	1,623,000
Actual Labor & Fringe	1,573,000
Savings	50,000
Target Spoilage & Reclamation (3.34%)	334,000
Actual Spoilage & Reclamation	294,000
Savings	40,000
Target Operating Supplies (4.00%)	400,000
Actual Operating Supplies	370,000
Savings	30,000
Total All Savings	120,000
Less: Deficit Reserve Contribution (33-1/3%)	40,000
Available for Distribution	80,000
Employee Share (65%)	52,000
Participating Payroll	$1,000,000
% of Participating Payroll	5.2%

age, scrap, and reclamation), and operating supplies. Each of these cost areas is measured separately and then aggregated to determine the value of the bonus pool.

The Dresser-Rand plan also deviates from the traditional multi-cost ratio in that there is a 7% cap on the payout. Bonuses in excess of 7% are not lost, however, but are added to the deficit reserve account for possible payout at year-end.

Distribution Center

A service industry example of a Multi-Cost Ratio with some twists is provided by a large distribution center. Their formula, with hypothetical data, is presented in Table 7-6.

This program, a pilot for the parent company, focuses on "controllable costs," which are identified as such on the income statement of the distribution center. This category essentially includes all operating costs except depreciation.

Table 7–6

Distribution Center

Gain Sharing Formula

Costs/Disbursements - Plan	10.92%
Costs/Disbursements - Actual	10.14%
Improvement	0.78%
Gain (0.78% × $75,792,000)	$591,178
Employee Share (25%)	147,795
Less: Quality Penalty (10%)	14,780
Net Employee Share	$133,015
Hours Worked	461,926
$/Hour	$0.29

Controllable costs are expressed as a percentage of "disbursements," which is the sales value of merchandise shipped. Because of difficult competitive circumstances, the company chose to use as its baseline the ratio of controllable costs in its annual profit plan rather than the actual ratio for a prior period. This ensured that bonuses would be paid only if cost performance was better than that required to meet the budget. Improvements are shared quarterly, with 25% distributed to the center's employees, both salaried and hourly.

To maintain a focus on service levels, the plan included a *quality modifier,* based on a survey of the distribution center's customers. Several thousand postcards are sent to customers each quarter, soliciting their responses to a small number of simple questions regarding the accuracy, condition, and timeliness of the shipments. If the average percentage of positive responses does not meet a predetermined level, up to 10% of the employee bonus pool is withheld.

This plan thus represents an important enhancement to the multi-cost formula by ensuring that customer satisfaction directly impacts employees' bonuses.

Chrysler Corporation

An organization that has modified the multi-cost ratio to eliminate the price effect is Acustar, Inc. a subsidiary of Chrysler. One example is the gain sharing plan at the company's plant in Evart, Michigan. Launched in 1988, this plan used an allowed cost ratio that was applied to *standard cost of sales* rather than to sales value of production. This approach effectively eliminated the impact of selling price on the gain sharing formula. At the same time, it raised a complication: standards change each year, and to the extent that improvements in the various cost elements were realized in a given year, the lower standard for the following year would result in lower allowed costs. This would undermine management's intentions to share improvements for a longer period than the year in which they occurred. Evart's solution was to adjust standard cost of sales each year so that the number better reflected the standards that existed in the year of the plan launch.

The trade-off, then, for eliminating the price effect was a more complicated formula. The effective use of Scanlon-type suggestion committees apparently offset this drawback, however, as the plan was credited with fostering significant cost improvements during its first two years.

As an interesting sidelight, the Evart plan also has a second formula, one that compares total plant hours worked to standard direct labor hours earned. This then represents an example of a gain sharing plan that uses both a physical productivity formula and a financial formula.

Still another twist on the multi-cost idea is employed at an Acustar plant in Dayton, Ohio. The plant has 1400 employees and is represented by the International Union of Electronic, Electrical, Salaried, Machine, and Furniture Workers (IUE).

Facing severe competitive pressures, management and union leaders at the Dayton plant agreed during 1988 contract discussions to adopt a "shared destiny" strategy. The agreement that resulted incorporated fewer job classifications, greater work force flexibility, and changes in past practices that had adversely affected productivity and quality. The agreement also provided for gain sharing as a replacement for more traditional forms of compensation.

The resulting formula, which was developed by a joint committee after the contract was ratified, used an allowed expense ratio based on *direct labor dollars earned* rather than on sales value of production. This particular variable is a measure of output obtained by multiplying the units of production for the period by the appropriate direct labor standard, in dollars. To ensure a consistent quantification of output over time, 1989 standards are used in all subsequent years.

The Chrysler plan at Dayton has add-on bonus opportunities as well. These are related to quantifiable improvements resulting from suggestions and reductions in absenteeism.

Miami Paper Corporation

Another variation that removes the effect of selling price on gain sharing bonuses is provided by Miami Paper Corporation, located in Miamisburg, Ohio. The company is a subsidiary of Pentair, Inc., a $1.2 billion company with operations in paper, auto parts, power tools, and lubrication systems.

The gain sharing plan was an outcome of a process undertaken by Miami Paper to change the role of employees by increasing their understanding of, commitment to, and involvement in the business. The process involved the positioning of each shift as a separate business unit, with business performance tracked by unit and communicated to employees. The change was accompanied by extensive technical and business training and supportive reward systems—an all-salaried work force and gain sharing. As stated in the plan document, "Miami Paper's Gain Sharing Plan was designed to enhance the Team Concept in an effort to merge personal and organizational goals."

As in the standard approach to the Multi-Cost Ratio, the gain sharing system measures a variety of expenses that employees can influence. These expenses, as spelled out in the plan document, are shown in Table 7-7.

This formula varies, however, from the typical approach used to determine allowed expenses. Rather than using an allowed ratio to sales or sales value of production, Miami Paper uses an *allowed cost per ton.* As in the Chrysler Acustar examples, the effect of selling price is removed from the equation. In contrast to the Chrysler plans, there is no necessity to deal with changing standards.

The program also deviates from the usual multi-cost formula in another way: it incorporates explicit indicators of quality and safety. In contrast to the costs itemized in Table 7-7, which generally vary with volume, the quality and safety measures result in the addition of fixed amounts of costs to the actual cost total.

The quality indicator is *number of claims,* with each claim in excess of an allowed number adding $2,000 to costs. Safety is mea-

Table 7–7
Miami Paper Corporation
Included Expenses

Direct Labor, Base	Direct Labor, Double
Direct Labor, 1½	Salaries, Base
Salaries, Overtime	Repairs, Accuray Parts
Repairs, Equipment	Repairs, Lift Trucks
Repairs, OSHA	Repairs, Roll Grinding
Repairs, Electrical	Repairs, Elevators
Repairs, Walls/Doors	Supplies, Misc. Chemical
Supplies, Data Processing	Supplies, Fiber Cores
Supplies, Expendables	Supplies, Instruments
Supplies, Inventory Adj.	Supplies, Lubricants
Supplies, Lumber	Supplies, Minor Tools
Supplies, Piping	Supplies, Ref. Plates
Supplies, Safety	Supplies, Splice Tapes
Supplies, Wrappers	Supplies, Wet Felts
Supplies, Wires	Supplies, Dryer Felts
Supplies, Stores Cap.	Travel, Meals
Travel, Lodging	Travel, Misc.
Travel, Transportation	Travel, Entertainment
Travel, Business Exp.	Telephone
Demurrage	Utilities, Electrical
Water	Raw Material
Steam Fuel Usage	Quality Claim $

sured through two indicators: *lost-time accidents* and *OSHA record-able incidents.* Every lost-time accident adds $20,000 to measured costs for the period, and each OSHA recordable in excess of five per month adds $2,500 to costs.

The Miami Paper plan has yet another creative feature: additional payouts for the *achievement of records.* For each plant record achieved in production, quality, or other performance measures, up to six per quarter, $500 is added to the bonus pool.

The full calculation of the Miami Paper formula, with hypothetical numbers, is shown in Table 7-8.

Miami Paper is an excellent example of a company that has not allowed itself to be limited by the usual or standard approaches to gain sharing. It has instead added new dimensions to the straight-forward, but somewhat limited, multi-cost ratio.

Table 7–8
Miami Paper Corporation
Gain Sharing Formula

Variable Expenses:		
Total compensation		$1,280,300
Total repairs		146,800
Total supplies		393,000
Total travel		18,500
Telephone		12,900
Demurrage		3,100
Water		7,600
Electric utilities		184,300
Raw materials		6,032,600
Steam usage		160,400
Quality claims ($)		82,100
Fixed Expenses:		
# of quality claims @ $2,000		42,000
# of OSHA recordables @ $2,500		7,500
# of lost-time accidents @ $20,000		0
Total Expenses		8,371,100
Allowed Variable Expenses:		
Tons produced	11,750	
Allowed cost per ton	$728.40	8,558,700
Allowed fixed expenses		68,000
Total Allowed Expenses		8,626,700
Gain		255,600
Employee Share @ 50%		127,800
Records Set		2,000
Amount to be Distributed		129,800

Xerox Corporation

Still another variation on the multi-cost theme can be found at Xerox Corporation. Here again, quality, in the form of customer service, plays a key role in a financial formula in the service side of the business. There can be little doubt that Xerox is a quality-driven company, as they were a 1989 recipient of the Malcolm Baldrige National Quality Award.

Xerox's current quality and employee involvement strategies date back to the early 1980s, when the Japanese and other competitors began to make serious inroads into the company's market share in plain-paper copiers. The company recognized early on that the massive cultural change needed to meet these competitive challenges must also be accompanied by changes in the reward system.

The initial pilot gain sharing program was designed by a cross-functional management group in the company's U.S. customer service activity, which is responsible for maintaining the company's installed base of equipment. The service function consisted of 15,000 employees in 96 locations across the country. The initial test involved four locations.

To evaluate the success of the pilot gain sharing programs, performance in these four test districts was compared to that of twelve control districts with similar business characteristics.

The conclusion, after one year, was that gain sharing was successful in three of the test districts but did not meet expectations in the other one. A company analysis identified the results in the three successful locations. The results were:

◇ Dramatic revenue improvements over the control districts.
◇ Improvements in a variety of business indicators, such as expenses and customer satisfaction.
◇ Greater levels of employee involvement.
◇ Increased cross-functional cooperation and sharing of resources.
◇ Significant improvements in employee perceptions (as measured by a survey and employee roundtables) in such areas as ability to influence decisions and team meeting effectiveness.

Of equal interest are the findings from the location that did not realize significant improvements. Among other things, it was determined that the unsuccessful district made no serious attempt to change organizational behaviors. There was no real involvement, and managers were not prepared for a change to a participative style. The company made an interesting observation: installing gain sharing where real participation is absent causes organizational stress because employees will challenge management's decision-making style.

Following further tests and several changes to the plan design, gain sharing was launched nationwide in the customer service organization in 1989. The formula used was a simple one: expenses as a percent of revenue. The resulting ratio has to compare favorably to the one contained in the profit plan in order for there to be a gain sharing pool. Each district is measured as a separate entity, and payouts are made quarterly.

While the pool was split 50/50 between the company and the employees in the test programs, the employee share was reduced to 30% when the plan went national. The primary reason for this change was that the national plan used a broader measure with greater potential gains. This modification was also deemed necessary because of the possibility that gains achieved in successful districts could be partially or fully offset by losses in unsuccessful districts. The net effect of that scenario would be that bonuses on a national basis could represent a very high percentage (or even exceed) the overall gains.

The customer satisfaction feature alluded to earlier is a "gate": customer satisfaction ratings, as measured through a survey, must not fall below 96% of the plan level or no bonuses would be paid.

Going into 1991, Xerox is continuing its plan in the customer service organization and is also testing a variation to fit a major reorganization in 1988 that brought together customer service, marketing, and business operations in each district into a cross-functional business partnership. If the test is successful, the new program will tie bonuses to the profitability of these larger business enterprises.

Summary

Financial formulas, which are those denominated in dollars, represent the second major category of gain sharing measures. Unlike physical productivity formulas, financial formulas are generally influenced by various marketplace forces. They thus are normally associated with a Common Fate philosophy of compensation.

The best-known financial formula is the Scanlon plan, which rewards (in its traditional form) improvements in the ratio of payroll costs to sales value of production. More recently, the Scanlon formula has been modified to include a wide variety of costs in addition to labor. Another standardized approach that incorporates additional costs in the formula is the Rucker Plan®, which compares payroll costs to value added rather than to sales value of production.

Profit sharing plans, which meet our definition of gain sharing if cash payouts are made, represent the ultimate financial formula. The major weakness of profit sharing—it is not meaningful to most employees—can be ameliorated somewhat by making profit sharing bonuses contingent upon the achievement of more controllable improvements.

There are many examples of creative modifications to the more traditional financial formulas. Some of these modifications are designed to eliminate the effect of selling price changes on bonuses, while others serve to incorporate into the formula non-cost indicators such as safety and customer satisfaction.

References

1. McGregor, Douglas, *The Human Side of Enterprise.* New York: McGraw-Hill Book Company, 1960.
2. "Labor-Management Cooperation Brief: Employee Involvement and Gain Sharing Produce Dramatic Results at Eggers Industries." Washington, D.C.: U.S. Department of Labor, Bureau of Labor-Management Relations and Cooperative Programs, 1985.

Chapter 8

The Family of Measures

The third category of gain sharing formulas is of more recent vintage than the first two. Financial formulas—Scanlon, Rucker®, and profit sharing—have been around since the early days of gain sharing. Physical productivity formulas—IMPROSHARE® and its variants—go back at least 15 to 20 years.

The family of measures approach, on the other hand, is a relative infant in the gain sharing world; one would have been hard pressed to find examples prior to the 1980s. Its use is now growing rapidly, however, as it possesses certain advantages over its physical and financial cousins.

Basically, the family of measures category describes any gain sharing formula that uses *multiple, independent measures*. A gain (or loss) is calculated for each measure separately, and then aggregated to determine the size of the bonus pool.

The main attractions of the family of measures are flexibility and focus. This category is flexible in that a gain sharing plan can be built around any performance variables that are important to the success of the business. If, for example, the business strategy requires improvement in labor productivity, quality, materials utilization, and customer service, a family of measures formula could be constructed around those four specific components.

With a family of measures, the range of possible performance variables is much broader than it is with the other two categories. Physical productivity formulas are limited to just that; financial formulas are much broader but are still basically limited to rewarding improvements in costs. Family of measures programs, on the other hand, have been structured to explicitly reward quality, safety, delivery performance, attendance, employee involvement, customer satisfaction, and a variety of other variables. Clearly, these non-cost items cannot be as easily emphasized with the other gain sharing categories.

Apart from the inherent flexibility, the family of measures provides a greater opportunity to focus on improved performance than is possible with a financial measure. Financial formulas can be quite broad in scope (profit-sharing is a reflection of everything that happens in the business), but the focus is diffused. The measure may be affected by too many things, and employees may not have a clear sense of what they need to do in order to earn gain sharing bonuses. With a family of measures, the company can be quite specific about what types of improvements will yield bonuses.

These advantages do not come without a cost—the design process for a family of measures program is generally more time-consuming and complicated than it is for the other categories. The design team has to sort through a welter of potential performance variables and must consider various design issues a number of times—once for each variable selected to be included in the formula. The implementation and communication requirements can also be expected to be greater as well.

Auto Parts Manufacturer

A simple example of the family of measures approach is provided by a plant that manufactures automotive components. The plan was developed by a joint labor-management design team consisting of an equal number of management people and members of the local union.

The plant had been the first site in the company to implement a formal employee involvement program. As a result of that process, a committee was formed to investigate gain sharing, and ultimately the labor-management design team was formed.

The plan uses four measures: labor cost, scrap, operating supplies, and slug utilization (re-use of leftover steel after components have been cut by punch presses). The specific measures are shown in Table 8-1.

The baseline against which the measures are compared is the average of the three previous years. Gains are shared 50/50 between the company and employees, with bonuses paid quarterly. Bonuses are distributed to employees based on hours worked. Further discussion of these design features will be found in subsequent chapters.

The plan contains an additional feature that is somewhat unusual: any negative inventory adjustments resulting from the annual physical inventory are deducted from the bonus pool. Deductions are made quarterly, based on the previous year's adjustment; the deduc-

Table 8–1

Auto Parts Manufacturer
Gain Sharing Measures

Labor: Labor and fringe costs as percentage of throughput (sales minus material cost of sales)

Scrap: Scrap dollars as percentage of production cost.

Operating Supplies: Supplies and services as percentage of throughput

Slug Utilization: Standard cost of slugs utilized as percentage of standard cost of steel used.

tion for the final quarter reconciles the full year deductions to the actual inventory adjustment.

The plan is a straightforward illustration of the family of measures approach. Employee efforts are focused on a small number of specific, controllable variables, and it is likely that most employees are quite clear on what is being rewarded. The plan is considerably broader than one that is limited to labor productivity, yet there is greater line of sight than could probably be obtained through a financial formula.

Air Conditioner Manufacturer

A manufacturer of air conditioning equipment launched a pilot gain sharing plan at one of its plants in 1989.

The plan, which was the product of a joint design effort by management and the union, contained six measures, as summarized in Table 8-2.

The first three measures shown in the table are basic cost measures—labor, materials, and supplies. The labor measure (plant efficiency) uses an approach similar to that of the 3M Company—weighting units of output by a factor that reflects differences in labor content (Chapter 6). Both hourly and salaried hours are included in the denominator.

The schedule attainment measure is an excellent example of the use of a family of measures to reinforce important non-cost issues. The measure itself is a creative variation on the usual schedule attainment measure—percentage of scheduled units completed. By multiplying units missed by the number of weeks past due, the past due units carry an ever-increasing penalty to the gain sharing bonus until they are completed.

Table 8–2

Air Conditioner Manufacturer
Gain Sharing Measures

Plant Efficiency: $\dfrac{\text{Units produced} \times \text{equivalency factor}}{\text{Total hours worked}}$

Material Utilization: $\dfrac{\text{Standard material value of finished goods}}{\text{Material utilized}}$

Supplies Efficiency: $\dfrac{\text{Standard cost of goods produced}}{\text{Supply purchases}}$

Schedule Attainment: $\dfrac{\text{Actual Scheduled Production} - (\text{Missed units} \times \text{weeks past due})}{\text{Scheduled production}}$

Safety: OSHA frequency and severity measures

Quality: $\dfrac{\text{Total violation points}}{\text{No. of units audited}}$

A common concern expressed by gain sharing designers is how to value, for bonus purposes, gains in non-cost measures such as schedule attainment. One method is to establish an arbitrary value; for example, $1,000 might be added to the bonus pool for each percentage point improvement in schedule attainment. This arbitrary value must, of course, bear some reasonable semblance to management's judgment of what the improvement in question is worth to the company.

The company takes a different approach to valuing improvements in schedule attainment. The amount contributed to the bonus pool is based on the savings in inventory carrying cost realized through improvements in schedule performance. The company recognizes, however, that the more important gains lie in improved customer satisfaction.

Safety is measured in this system using two readily available indicators: the OSHA frequency (number of accidents × 1,000,000/total hours worked) and severity (number of days lost × 1,000,000/total hours worked) indicators.

The final gain sharing variable is quality, as measured through an already existing audit by divisional quality professionals. The outcome of the quality audit is an assessment of violation points based on the type and number of product defects found in the course of the audit process. These violation points are divided by the number of units audited to obtain a quality rating.

The quality indicator is used in a different manner than the other measures. Rather than adding dollars to the bonus pool based on calculated savings, it is used instead as a modifier: the total gains from the other measures are multiplied by the quality modifier to determine the size of the bonus pool. The value of the modifier is determined by comparing the quality rating to the plant's quality goal; some selected modifier levels are shown in Table 8-3.

Table 8–3

**Air Conditioner Manufacturer
Quality Modifier**

Quality Rating as % of Plant Goal	Bonus Pool Modifier
78%	0%
80	10
85	35
90	60
95	90
98	100
100	110

Using quality as a modifier elevates that variable to a higher level of influence than it would command if it were simply one of several measures that contributed absolute dollars to the bonus pool. As a modifier, it has the power to dramatically reduce, or even eliminate, all of the gains achieved through the other variables. This design feature thus fits well with an organizational emphasis on quality improvement.

This plan contains another feature of interest: if the safety measures exceed the goal, the pool associated with that measure (two hours per month per employee × the average hourly wage rate) would be paid out regardless of the outcome on all of the other measures. In other words, losses on the other variables, or a poor quality performance, cannot reduce the safety bonus. Management is clearly sending an important message: safety stands alone and will be rewarded as an end in itself.

With the exception of the schedule attainment and quality variables, which are tied to the achievement of targets, the plan uses an eight-quarter rolling baseline (the baseline equals the average of the last eight quarters' performance). Gains are shared 50/50, and paid quarterly.

The complete payout calculation for the plan is summarized in Table 8-4.

Table 8–4

Air Conditioner Manufacturer
Payout Calculation

	Material Utilization Savings
+	Plant Efficiency Savings
+	Supplies Efficiency Savings
+	Schedule Attainment Savings
=	Total Savings
×	Quality Modifier
=	Total Gain
×	50% Employee Share
=	Employee Share of Gains
+	Safety Pool
=	Total Employee Bonus Pool

Computer Services

A useful example of a family of measures in a service industry is provided by the Business Management Services Division (BMSD) of Control Data Corporation. BMSD provides computerized human resources, payroll, and related services to external customers through a network of 40 sales and service centers.

BMSD management, recognizing the importance of quality and customer service to the success of their business, developed a business strategy to increase the focus on the customer. Gain sharing was viewed as a key element to obtain employee commitment to and involvement in the quality improvement process.

There were virtually no models for gain sharing in the computer services business, and with 40 offices providing essentially identical services, it made sense to pilot a gain sharing program in one office initially. The Southfield, Michigan center was chosen, largely because it was one of the highest performing locations. The program was launched at the beginning of 1990.

The system was developed by an employee design team at the Southfield facility, and is noteworthy for the use of some unusual measures, which are summarized in Table 8-5.

Table 8–5
Control Data Business Management Services
Gain Sharing Measures

Number of credits issued
Retention of customers
Cost per processing
Controllable expenses as % of revenues
Number of suggestions submitted

Two of the gain sharing measures, cost per processing and controllable expenses, are straightforward cost measures. Of greater interest are the other measures, which focus on quality and customer satisfaction.

It was imperative that the system incorporate an indicator of quality, and after much consideration, the design team selected the *number of credits issued,* a measure that is probably unique in the gain sharing arena. The reasoning for this choice was simple: any time a credit has to be issued, someone has made a mistake and the customer is probably unhappy. The customer may not have been provided the full service he was entitled to, or he may have been quoted an incorrect price by the salesperson. Perhaps the invoice simply contained an arithmetic or clerical error of some kind. In any event, credits represent a broad array of quality problems and thus have no place in a total quality process.

In order to use this indicator, the gain associated with the reduction of credits issued had to be determined. While the intent of this plan was to improve quality and customer satisfaction, the financial gains resulting from improvements in these variables were indeterminable. Accordingly, the design team decided that bonuses should be based on the cost savings that resulted from handling fewer credits. An analysis of the administrative effort required to issue a credit concluded that each credit costs $80 to process. This amount was thus added to the bonus pool for each unit reduction in the number of credits issued.

Another interesting measure in the Control Data plan is *customer retention.* Invariably, a certain number of customers are lost each year, some to other vendors, some because of a decision by the customer to process their payroll in-house. Clearly, retaining customers is important to the growth and success of the business and should be an outcome of higher customer satisfaction. Therefore, the profit effect of retaining a greater percentage of customers than was accomplished in the base period is credited to the gain sharing pool.

The last of the family of measures is an indicator of employee involvement in the improvement process itself. For each suggestion submitted to the company suggestion plan (up to a maximum of ten per quarter), $100 is added to the bonus pool. The suggestion must be approved for submission by the local suggestion program coordinator and it must have been developed by a team, rather than by an individual, in order to qualify for gain sharing credit. In addition, if the suggestion is ultimately approved by the corporation (which means there are potential savings in 40 offices), an additional $100 is added to the bonus pool.

The Control Data plan also has two modifiers—variables that can add to, reduce, or even eliminate the overall bonus pool. One is based on the gross profits of the unit, a fairly common approach that is discussed in more detail in Chapter 10. The other modifier is based on a *survey of customer satisfaction.*

The survey process is called the CARE (Customers Are Really Essential) Program. The surveys are conducted by telephone, and customers are requested to answer a series of questions, with responses ranging from "poor" to "excellent." The percentage of excellent responses is used to modify the gain sharing pool, as shown in Table 8-6.

A customer satisfaction measure would seem to be a natural for a company that wants to integrate its gain sharing program into a total quality process. However, the imprecision of a survey troubles many managers, particularly those with a bent towards precise quantification of the variables to which pay is to be tied. Nonetheless, the only way to directly gauge customer satisfaction is to ask the customer, and the use of survey results as gain sharing measures or modifiers is growing.

Table 8–6
Control Data
Care Program Modifier

% Excellent Responses	Adjustment to Pool
100%	+15%
99	+12
98	+9
97	+6
96	+3
95	0
94	–3
93	–6
92	–9
91	–12
90	–15

The Control Data program, in summary, is of interest for two reasons: it is one of the few examples of a family of measures approach in a service business, and it plows some new ground in the creative use of quality measures.

Goal-Based Systems

Up to this point, all of the gain sharing examples reviewed involved a consistent approach to determining payouts: gains are quantified, and a portion of those gains are paid back to participating employees. While this is indeed the predominate model, there is another way: paying a predetermined amount for the *achievement of goals.*

In this approach, a goal is established for each of the measures, and a fixed dollar amount (or per cent) is paid to employees for each goal that is achieved.

Goal-based gain sharing systems have some advantages that are worth considering:

◊ They are simpler to design. Design teams are relieved of making decisions around several design components. They don't have to establish a baseline, a task which can require a good deal of analytical work. They don't have to worry about an explicit share. And the same rigor is simply not necessary when evaluating and selecting measures to be used in the formula.

◊ They can be tied to existing organizational goals, thus increasing the visibility of and commitment to those goals.
◊ The maximum payout is known in advance. Payouts cannot exceed the amount that would be awarded if all the goals are achieved; this may provide some comfort to management people who are concerned about the possibility of "runaway" payouts. This comfort can be provided in a more conventional gain sharing system by simply capping the payout; however, as we shall see in Chapter 11, caps may be undesirable for other reasons.

As with everything else in gain sharing, we must also consider the potential disadvantages of goal-based systems:

◊ The plan may have lower credibility with employees. This is particularly true if the goals established do not appear reasonable to employees. In their view, management may be manipulating them by setting almost unreachable targets and providing only token rewards for achieving them. This particular pitfall can be ameliorated, of course, by involving employees in the development of the goals.
◊ Improvements may be limited. While management limits the potential payout, it may also be limiting the potential improvement. Once the goal has been achieved, there is no motivation to continue to improve beyond that level.
◊ Improvements that fall short of the goal are not rewarded. This event could well result in frustration and dissatisfaction with the program. This problem, as well as the previous one, can be lessened by having multiple goal levels.

A company considering the use of a goal-based gain sharing program should, of course, weigh the risks against the benefits before making a decision.

Arco Chemical Company

Arco Chemical's Bayport plant in the Houston area launched its gain sharing program in 1985. This initial effort, which was structured around annual goals, did not succeed because business conditions at the time rendered the goals unachievable. The program was modified the following year to incorporate monthly goals as well as annual goals into the system.

The 1989 program included seventeen monthly goals and three annual goals, with points awarded for the achievement of each goal. The 1989 goals, many of which are technical and probably meaningful only to people in the chemical industry, and associated points are detailed in Table 8-7.

Table 8–7
Arco Chemical Company
1989 Goals

Monthly Goals	Max Points Per Month	Max Points Per Year
Propylene yield	6	72
Isobutane yield	6	72
Steam consumption	2	24
Losses to fuel gas	3	36
On-stream time	4	48
Computer loop uptime	1	12
MMS processing	1	12
TBHP quality	1	12
Po Test Tank Samples	2	24
Glycol quality	1	12
PO(E) production	5	60
PO(E) production daily average	5	60
Glycols production	1	12
Customer complaints	2	24
Recordable cases	2	24
Gulf coast waste disposal	2	24
TBA pipeline quality	2	24
Quality charting	2	24

Annual Goals		
Attendance		
a) First tier		50
b) Second tier		10
Lost time accidents		24

The maximum number of points that can be earned under Arco Chemical's program is 522, with each point worth .0158% of employees' pay. Simple arithmetic shows that the maximum bonus potential is thus 8.25%. All permanent employees are eligible.

The goal set includes a number of non-cost items, such as safety (recordable cases) and attendance. There are actually two attendance goals; the first tier goal in 1989 was to achieve an absentee rate of 0.95% or better, while the second tier goal was to beat the plant's record attendance of 0.67%. It should be noted that achievement of the attendance goal would result in the appropriate payout to all employees, regardless of their individual attendance record. This practice, while objectionable to some, is perfectly in keeping with the principle that a group incentive such as gain sharing should not differentiate among individual contributions.

Another interesting and unusual goal is the one for *quality charting*. In essence, achievement of this goal required that all work areas have meaningful statistical process control or quality charts. Here is another reinforcement for the idea that gain sharing need not be limited to traditional performance measures of productivity and cost.

The company has reported as much as $3 million in annual gains from this program.

Duke Power Company

A goal-based family of measures plan can also be useful for a company-wide program. In fact, it may be the only realistic alternative to profit sharing for a sizeable company that wishes to have all employees covered under a single bonus pool. One of the pioneers with this approach was Duke Power Company, an electric utility headquartered in Charlotte, North Carolina.

Duke Power introduced its Employee Incentive Goals Program in 1981. Each year, corporate management establishes a series of corporate goals; the total can vary, but usually numbers between eight and ten. The goals selected for 1990 are shown in Table 8-8.

Due to regulatory considerations, Duke Power chose to pay gain sharing bonuses as matching contributions to the Employee Stock Purchase-Savings Program. Under this program, an employee may contribute up to 10% of his salary toward the purchase of company stock. The stock purchased accumulates in the employee's account until retirement.

Table 8–8

Duke Power Company

1990 Gain Sharing Goals

Employee safety—lost time accidents
Employee safety—vehicle accidents
Customer service (outage minutes per customer)
Affirmative action
Electricity sales
Energy management (peak load reductions)
Efficient fossil production (heat rate generated by fossil plants)
Nuclear production (nuclear system capacity)

If four of the eight goals are achieved, the company will make a 24% matching contribution. For each goal achieved beyond four, the company contributes another 6%. Goal number five carries an additional 2% match.

There is also a bonus goal, which can add an additional 10% of the employee contribution. This award is based on controlling costs by staying within budget and is independent of the other eight goals.

It is readily apparent that all of the goals cannot be meaningful to all employees. Certain goals, for example, apply primarily to power plant employees. In a single plan covering several thousand employees, it is surely unrealistic to expect to construct a family of measures in which all measures are meaningful to all employees.

Duke Power has taken care, however, to ensure that all employees can relate to at least one of the measures. Every employee can presumably focus on improving something that is important to the success of the business.

It should also be noted that all employees receive the bonus for each goal achieved, whether or not they had any direct opportunity to contribute to that result. This feature reinforces the idea that all employees are part of the company team, with their financial well-being tied to the success of the business.

Formula Selection Criteria

Having reviewed the various formula categories in the last three chapters, the natural question is, "How does one choose among the various categories and select specific measures?" The criteria to consider are:

◇ Conformity with management philosophy. Does management believe employees should be rewarded for things they directly control, or does management want employees' pay tied to the success of the business? This is probably the key question relative to formula category selection. The Controllability advocates will adopt a physical productivity formula, while those of the Common Fate persuasion will opt for a financial formula. A family of measures, of course, can be tailored for either philosophy.

◇ Importance to business success. Measuring variables that are not important to the success of the business would be a critical error, as the resulting increase in compensation will not be accompanied by concomitant benefits to the company. Sometimes management, in their desire to measure only factors that are totally controllable by employees, eliminate from consideration the most important business variables and are left with relatively inconsequential items.

◇ Perception of fairness. If employees do not believe the gain sharing program is a fair and equitable compensation system, it will probably not meet expectations. Care should be taken, therefore, to ensure that indicators selected are reasonably accurate measures of the variable in question, are not subject to undue distortion, and will reflect any employee efforts to improve them.

◇ Controllability by employees. While the Common Fate philosophy allows for measures that are influenced by external events, there still must be a substantial element of controllability in the plan. If the measures are totally out of the control of employees, there is no motivational effect and no reason for employees to change their behaviors. One company in a commodity-type business tied bonuses to the selling price of the product; they got variable compensation, but it did nothing for employee involvement or cultural change.

◇ Simplicity. Unless the organization is populated by rocket scientists, the measures should be kept as simple as possible. If people do not understand what is being measured, or the measures lack credibility because they are too complicated to comprehend, the effectiveness of the program will suffer. This does not necessarily mean that all employees must fully understand the precise arithmetic underlying the measures; that is probably too high an expectation in a complicated business. It does mean, however, that employees are clear about *what* is being measured and have a reasonable level of trust in the validity of the measures.

◇ Comprehensive. In addition to being an effective method for improving labor productivity, gain sharing should be viewed as an effective vehicle for improving other variables that employees can influence such as quality, material utilization, schedule compliance, and customer satisfaction. A company that uses gain sharing to reward only a single, narrow performance factor is probably missing a significant opportunity.

Summary

The family of measures, the third category of gain sharing formula, is of more recent vintage than the other two categories and offers certain advantages. Because it consists of multiple performance measures, it provides a means to tie bonuses to a variety of performance variables beyond simple productivity. At the same time, it generally fosters greater organizational focus on the key variables, with a greater degree of controllability, than can be achieved with a financial measure. The trade-off for these advantages is a more lengthy and difficult design process.

The family of measures approach also offers great flexibility and opportunity for creativity. Variables such as quality, safety, and customer satisfaction are easily accommodated in this formula approach.

The ultimate choice of a formula category, as well as the specific measures themselves, is dependent on a number of considerations, including management's compensation philosophy and key business needs.

Chapter 9

The Baseline

Before a company can share gains, it clearly must answer the question, "Gains versus what?"

There are really two design issues to deal with here. The obvious one involves the initial establishment of a baseline value for the measure or measures. A company simply cannot quantify a gain without it. The second design decision relates to the manner in which the baseline will change in future periods. Baseline decisions are far from trivial, as they determine the level of payout and have a great bearing on the perceived fairness of the gain sharing system.

Setting the Baseline

Baselines can be classified into two basic categories, with many variants of each. *Historical baselines* cover all those baselines that reflect some past level of performance. *Target baselines* describe those baselines that are established at some level that exceeds previous performance levels.

Survey data suggest that the majority of gain sharing programs, about 60%, use historical baselines.[1] The primary attraction of the historical baseline is credibility. With an historical baseline, the company shares with its employees any improvements in performance, from the first dollar. It therefore conforms with a management philosophy based on "partnership" with the company's employees. Participants in the gain sharing program are more likely to view an historical baseline as fair and equitable, and this increases the probability of their buying into the program.

There are, however, certain situational advantages to a target baseline:

◇ Recent history may be invalid as an indicator of the present status of the performance variable in question because of major changes in products, processes, technology, or volume.

◇ Where the organization is uncompetitive in its business or suffering financial difficulties, improvements over history simply may not be good enough to justify increasing compensation.

◇ Pay can be tied to the achievement of goals contained in a budget or strategic plan, thus increasing employees' awareness of these goals.

◇ In a new start-up operation, or where new measures are being used, there may be no history.

Like other design decisions in gain sharing, there are no right or wrong answers with regard to the baseline. Choices should be made based on considerations of philosophy, business circumstances, and equity.

Historical Baselines

Having opted for the historical baseline approach, the gain sharing designers must then decide what historical period to use. The time period selected could be as brief as the last quarter or as long as the average of three to five previous years.

A rational decision on this question cannot be made without collecting history for the measures in question and graphing the data. The two graphs in Figure 9-1 show three years of history, and end at the same level. The average for the period has been drawn on the graph in each case.

It would be perfectly reasonable to use the three-year average as the baseline in the case of the top graph. Performance has varied from period to period, but over the long run it has obviously been fairly stable. The three-year average is a good representation of the present status of this variable.

The bottom graph is a horse of a different color. Here too there are short-term variations, but more importantly, there is a clear underlying trend. The value of this variable has improved noticeably over the three-year period. Using the three-year average in this case would probably be a mistake, as the organization is presently well above that level. A company would be paying instant bonuses—perhaps large ones—even if no further improvement takes place; in effect, it would be sharing past improvements with employees. More than one company has fallen into this trap, and in some cases it has forced management to terminate the program.

Where a definite trend exists in the history, it would be wise to use a shorter period in establishing the baseline in order to better reflect

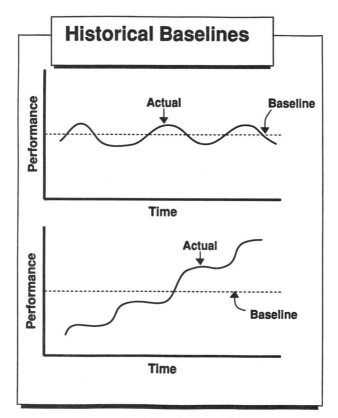

Figure 9-1. Historical Baselines.

the current performance level. Or, as an alternative, a target baseline could be adopted.

In a gain sharing program based on a family of measures, a question may arise regarding the need for a consistent baseline among all the measures. All other things being equal, it is generally desirable to have a consistent baseline treatment for all of the measures. However, consistency should not be forced to the detriment of the viability of the system, and it is not unusual for organizations to have different baseline periods for different measures. These decisions should be made based on a thorough study and understanding of the historical data underlying the various measures.

One concern often expressed by management when contemplating the baseline issue relates to their expectation that a certain amount of improvement in the measures will occur through management efforts alone. They will point, for example, to average annual increases in productivity of 5% over the last several years. These improvements were, of course, achieved without gain sharing. Doesn't an historical baseline, therefore, violate the self-funding principle in the sense that the company will be sharing a certain amount of gains that it would have obtained anyway?

This is a more complex question than it might appear on the surface. First of all, can management really be certain that it will continue to achieve its historical rate of improvement without the commitment and involvement of its employees? The United States enjoyed an average annual rate of productivity improvement of 3% for a twenty-year period following World War II. But that growth rate began to drop in the late sixties, and since then has barely exceeded 1% annually.[2] Many businesses in many industries have painfully learned that trends do not continue forever.

Perhaps more importantly, gain sharing may be a necessary ingredient to realize the full benefits of organizational change. If a company is trying to create a culture based on involvement, teamwork, and partnership, its reward system must signal management's commitment to this philosophy. If it does not share gains over historical performance, it risks sending an inappropriate signal, that is "We want our employees to be partners in the business, but only after management gets what it would get anyway without their help." Such a message, even if unintended, could well limit the progression of the involvement process and reduce the potential gains.

Whether an historical baseline is fully consistent with the self-funding principle is not easily determined by a simple yes or no answer. In fact, it is probably impossible to answer the question with any degree of certainty. The concern about self-funding with an historical baseline can be lessened somewhat through the use of a lower employee share of the gains than might otherwise be appropriate. (See Chapter 10.)

Target Baselines

If, for whatever reason, an historical baseline is not desired or appropriate, the alternative is the target baseline. In this case, a performance level that is *better* than recent history is established as the base against which improvement will be shared. The target can come from anywhere; the budget or profit plan is probably the most common source. Targets can also be established from production standards, competitive performance levels, or purely arbitrary improvement goals.

Target baselines are used in one of two ways. The first approach, as described in the discussion of goal-based systems in Chapter 8, provides for the payment of a predetermined amount if the target is hit. The second method shares all gains above the target level. An example of the latter approach is the distribution center system described in Chapter 7.

From a management point of view, the primary attraction of a target baseline is that the company gets a certain amount of "free" gains; bonus payments do not kick in until performance has advanced to a higher plane. This idea particularly appeals to the "we-would-get-some-improvement-anyway" school of thought described earlier.

When viewed from an employee perspective, on the other hand, this advantage becomes a detriment. It may appear to plan participants that management wants them to "jump through hoops" in return for modest recompense. It might also undermine management's assertions that it wants employees to be partners in the business.

Clearly, a critical factor for success with a target baseline is the credibility of the targets. They must appear to be reasonable goals, and the reward must be adequate to justify striving for the targets. Nothing, of course, can improve credibility more than the involvement of the plan participants in establishing the goals. A good example of this involvement is the plan at the Contech Division of Sealed Power Technologies described in Chapter 7.

Changing The Baseline

Having decided upon a baseline, the gain sharing designers might conclude that they are ready to move on to the next design component. This would be an unfortunate conclusion because it would leave unresolved a major design issue: how the baseline will *change* over time.

Nothing in a gain sharing plan should be left to interpretation or judgment at a later date. This guideline is particularly important with respect to the nature of the baseline change, for a seemingly arbitrary and unexpected decision to tighten the baseline and thus reduce or eliminate bonuses will surely undermine trust in management and the credibility of the gain sharing program. This unfortunate outcome should be precluded by clearly defining in advance how future baselines will be established.

We will review in turn three basic approaches to baseline change:

◇ Fixed baselines
◇ Ratcheting baselines
◇ Rolling baselines

Fixed Baselines

The more traditional gain sharing plans, such as Scanlon and Rucker®, are often characterized by baselines that do not routinely change over time. Once the baseline has been established, employees can expect it to remain at that level indefinitely. In an environment of continuous improvement, bonuses can be expected to increase over time with a fixed baseline, as shown in Figure 9-2.

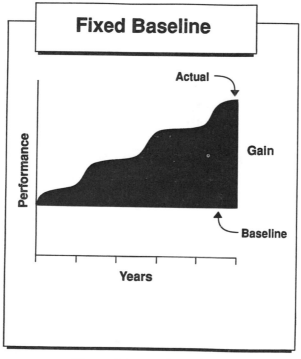

Figure 9-2. Fixed Baseline.

While fixed baselines do not *routinely* change, it does not mean that they *never* change. It would normally be important in a fixed baseline plan, for example, to provide for baseline changes to reflect the impact of major capital investments (this feature will be discussed in Chapter 11). In addition, some fixed baseline plans—IMPROSHARE®, most notably—cap the payout and adjust the baseline through a buy-back mechanism once the cap has been exceeded (also discussed in Chapter 11). Finally, it is important to maintain the flexibility to change the baseline if it should become meaningless due to major changes in the business, such as product line additions or deletions.

The fixed baseline, of course, is the most attractive option from the employees' point of view, as gains achieved in any given period will continue to generate bonuses indefinitely into the future. Those who favor the fixed baseline will argue that this is only fair because the company will continue to benefit from these gains in future years.

This argument is an oversimplification, however. It assumes that the company's share of the gains somehow flow into the pockets of managers or shareholders. While that could be the case in some circumstances, it is rather unlikely in a highly competitive environment. Where competition is intense, it is more likely that the company's share of the gains will flow to the *customer,* in the form of lower selling prices (or lower price increases). While the company is improving its performance through gain sharing, its competitors will not be standing still. They too will be attempting to lower their costs (some may even be astute enough to use gain sharing themselves), and they will likely pass on at least part of their gains to their customers in order to maintain or enhance their market share. If our hypothetical company simply keeps all of its gains, it may well lose its competitive position. Such an outcome surely would not be in the best interests of the company or its employees.

Apart from the above consideration, many gain sharing companies are concerned that a fixed baseline may be incompatible with a philosophy of *continuous improvement.* Employees whose pay continues to be enriched from years of past improvements may, they fear, be less motivated to tackle ever more difficult problems and challenges.

Some companies have chosen to modify their baseline annually for pricing, product mix, and capital changes only. This results, in effect, in a baseline that is fixed relative to performance improvement. An example of this approach can be found in the long-running Scanlon Plan at Atwood Industries.

If a fixed baseline is deemed to be inappropriate for whatever reason, then two alternative treatments remain.

Ratcheting Baselines

The antithesis of the fixed baseline is one that is reset each year to reflect the previous year's (or shorter period's) performance. In effect, the baseline "ratchets" up and therefore eliminates last year's gain from the current year's gain sharing arithmetic. Last year's gains are history; if bonuses are to be earned in the current year, entirely new gains must be generated. This situation is graphically depicted in Figure 9-3. The implications of the ratcheting baseline are readily apparent when Figure 9-3 is compared to Figure 9-2. Assuming the same amount of improvement over the years, the gain sharing pool will be much smaller under a ratcheting baseline scenario.

Figure 9-3. Ratcheting Baseline.

The mechanics of the ratcheting baseline are quite simple; all that is necessary is to calculate the average performance level for the gain sharing measures during the previous year. This figure then becomes the baseline for the current year.

Most goal-based gain sharing programs in effect have ratcheting baselines. In fact, because the goals usually represent performance levels that are *better* than the previous year, these systems can be called "super-ratchets."

Just as the employee will champion the fixed baseline, management can be expected to advocate the ratchet. It suits their conviction that employees should be rewarded for current contributions, not for past heroics. Assuming these different perceptions about what is fair with respect to baseline changes exists, how can these differences be reconciled?

One means of reconciliation lies in another design component, the Share. If employees must constantly improve on last year's performance in order to earn a bonus, it is only reasonable that they enjoy a relatively larger share of those gains than if they are compensated for previous years' gains as well. While a 25% employee share might be reasonable for a fixed-baseline program, it is probably inadequate (from an equity point of view) in a ratchet situation. Programs with ratcheting baselines are likely to have employee share ratios of 50% or greater.

The other means for reconciling the different perspectives (if they exist) lies in the third option for baseline changes: the rolling baseline.

Rolling Baselines

Like the ratcheting version, rolling baselines change on a regular basis. They differ in that the change is more gradual. Basically, a rolling baseline is one that reflects the average of several past years' performance.

Let's take as an example a three-year rolling baseline. At the beginning of each plan year, the new baseline would be established at a level equal to the average of the last three years' performance for the measures in question. The baseline is a rolling three-year average.

The rolling baseline often represents a satisfactory compromise between the conflicting views of management and employees. Management is satisfied because the baseline changes each year, and if improvement ceases, the bonus will ultimately disappear (it will take three years in the example cited above). Employees, on the other hand, enjoy the benefits of their improvement efforts for more than one year.

The length of the rolling period, of course, can be tailored to everyone's satisfaction. While three-year periods are common, there are also a number of examples of two-year rolling baselines, including St. Luke's Hospital in Kansas City (Chapter 6).

An increasingly common variant of the rolling baseline is one that averages several past *quarters*. The 3M Company (Chapter 6) uses a 12-quarter rolling baseline in its gain sharing plans. The baseline is thus adjusted every quarter, rather than annually. Control Data, in its pilot plan (Chapter 8) uses an eight-quarter rolling baseline.

A plan with a baseline that rolls on a quarterly basis is a tighter system than one that incorporates an annual roll, as gains that occur in any given quarter will immediately be reflected, at least partially, in the baseline. On the other hand, baseline changes are more gradual, which increases the stability of bonus payments. In a plan where the baseline changes annually, there may be a rather precipitous drop in bonus payments in the first period of the new year.

One question that inevitably arises from those considering a moving baseline is, "What happens when performance improvement flattens out as it approaches the maximum possible level?"

On the one hand, this scenario may be more theoretical than real. Many would argue that there is so much room for improvement in American industry that the likelihood of maximizing any performance variable in the foreseeable future is next to nil. And indeed, there are companies that have consistently improved productivity or other variables for many, many years.

Nonetheless, it is certainly conceivable that maximum or near-maximum performance could be achieved in some circumstances. A company can hardly improve on zero defects, for example, and a perfect safety record is tough to beat. Should it reach this wonderful state where little additional improvement is possible, it has two options. One is to refocus the gain sharing plan on other performance variables where there is room for improvement. The other option is to stop rolling the baseline, effectively converting it to a fixed baseline at a point somewhat below the current performance level. Employees could thus continue to earn a bonus for maintaining this extraordinary performance.

At least one company had the foresight to provide for this contingency in the design of its plan by specifying the level at which the rolling baseline would become fixed. St. Luke's Hospital had a similar thought in mind when it provided for "maintenance" bonuses to be paid to departments whose cost performance had become the best in the industry.

Summary

The baseline is a key gain sharing design component, for without it a company cannot quantify the gain. There are two major decisions to be made around the baseline.

The first decision is whether the baseline will reflect historical performance or will be a target. Historical baselines are the most common and, all other things being equal, are probably more credible to plan participants. There are circumstances, however, where an historical baseline may not be appropriate. History may not be a valid indicator of current performance levels, for example, or it may be unacceptable from a competitive point of view.

The second major decision involves the manner of baseline change over time. Fixed baselines do not routinely change so gains realized in a given year continue to be shared indefinitely. The other end of the spectrum is the ratcheting baseline, which eliminates from the gain sharing program all previously earned gains. A middle ground is the rolling baseline, which utilizes a moving average technique to share gains for a longer, but limited, period of time.

Because baseline decisions have a major bearing on the bonus-earning potential and perceived equity of a gain sharing program, they should not be made without careful thought and analysis.

References

1. O'Dell, Carla and McAdams, Jerry, *People, Performance, and Pay.* Houston, TX.: American Productivity and Quality Center, 1987.
2. Thor, Carl G., *Perspectives 90.* Houston, TX.: American Productivity and Quality Center, 1990.

Chapter 10

The Share,
The Frequency,
and The Split

Before a completed gain sharing system can be put in place, at least three additional design components must be considered. The Share (how the gains will be divided between the company and participating employees), the Frequency (how often gains will be paid out), and the Split (how the employee share of the gains will be distributed among the individual employees) are the minimum remaining issues that must be addressed before a functional gain sharing program can be put into practice. There also are some optional design components that are worth considering; these will be discussed in the next chapter.

The Share

Because gain sharing is not a discretionary system, but is based on a predetermined design, it is important to define in advance the proportion of the measured gain that will be paid to employees. The initial reaction of many people to this issue is that the share should be "50/50"—one-half retained by the company, one-half paid out to participating employees. The logic is that 50/50 "sounds fair," and that is certainly indisputable. And indeed, 50/50 is undoubtedly the single most common sharing arrangement.

The decision is not quite as simple as that, however, and the fact that 50/50 sounds fair doesn't necessarily make it right.

Share Criteria

In the vast majority of plans (profit sharing excepted), the employee share of the gains falls somewhere between 25% and 50%.

One can always find a few plans that award employees more than 50% of the gains—the most notable being the traditional, labor-only Scanlon Plan, which pays 75%—but they are the exception.

Perceived fairness is certainly an important criterion, and that accounts for the clustering at the high end of the 25-50% range. Some other criteria should be considered as well.

◇ Nature of the formula. The broader the formula, other things being equal, the lower the employee share should be. A broad formula, encompassing many different types of costs, offers greater potential gains than one that only rewards a single, narrow performance variable such as labor productivity. In the latter case, it may be necessary to pay a relatively high share of the gain to employees in order to ensure that the bonus potential is sufficient to provide an adequate incentive. In addition, a very broad formula, such as one that includes all operating costs, is approaching profit sharing in concept. And the more a plan resembles profit sharing, the smaller the employee share is likely to be. Companies are generally loathe to pay out a high percentage of profits, as this is also the source of funds for reinvestment and for rewarding the company's owners.

◇ Capital intensity of the business. Companies with high capital needs may feel a need to retain a large percentage of their gains in order to fund investment programs. In addition, capital-intensive businesses, such as those in the continuous process industries, tend to have a relatively small number of employees, thus allowing large bonuses to be paid with a relatively small employee share.

◇ Baseline decisions. If a company is to maintain a perception of equity, it cannot establish the share without considering the nature of the baseline. As a general principle, the more demanding the baseline, the higher should be the employee share. This means that a plan that shares improvements over a target should probably carry a higher employee share than one that employs an historical baseline. By the same token, a rolling or ratcheting baseline would justify a higher employee share than one that remains fixed. If the baseline features are not taken into account, the effort required to earn bonuses may be out of line with the sharing arrangement. For this reason, the share decision should normally be deferred until after baseline decisions have been made.

In some types of plans, the employee share is not explicit. In goal-based systems, where predetermined amounts are paid for the achievement of goals (see discussion of Arco Chemical in Chapter 8), there is no need for a defined share because the gain is not quantified. This does not mean, of course, that the plan designers can ignore this issue; the payout amount should not be arbitrary but should be based on an analysis of the gains that actually would be realized if the goals were achieved. Failure to do this, of course, could result in payouts that exceeded the gain itself. Or, at the other end of the spectrum, payouts might represent such a ridiculously small proportion of the gain that they are grossly inequitable. So while the company/employee share may not always be an explicitly defined component of the gain sharing plan, it must nonetheless be considered in the plan design.

The Variable Share

An innovative gain sharing design feature that has recently appeared on the scene and is growing rapidly is the variable share. Simply put, a variable share is an arrangement whereby the employee share of the gains is not predetermined but is based on the value of another variable. The other variable is most commonly a measure of profitability. The bonus pool is calculated in the usual way, and the pool is then divided between the company and its employees based on a table such as the generalized one shown in Table 10-1.

Table 10-1

Variable Share
Based on Profitability

Return on Investment	Employee Share of Gain
High	50%
Average	35
Low	20
Negative	0

The purpose of a variable share based on profitability (also called a profit modifier) is to ensure that high bonuses are not paid out to employees in times of low or non-existent profitability. The risk of this happening is most pronounced in controllability-oriented plans (see Chapter 5), where employees may be improving the gain sharing measures while the company is suffering financial setbacks due to market conditions or other uncontrollable events. But even in Common Fate financial plans, there may be substantial uncontrollable forces that are not fully reflected in the gain sharing formula. The variable share thus can serve as a safety valve, for any plan that consistently pays bonuses in the face of bottom-line losses risks eventual termination by management.

The profit modifier can take any number of forms. Rather than being tied to absolute levels of profitability, for example, the employee share may be adjusted based on profitability compared to a budget or profit plan. An example is the plan used by Control Data in its computer services business (Chapter 8). As shown in Table 10-2, the employee share in this plan is modified (up or down) based on the unit's gross profit performance to plan.

Table 10–2
Control Data
Business Management Services
Profit Modifier

Percent Gross Profit	Employee Share
More than 2 pct. points over Plan	50%
Between Plan and 2 pct. points over Plan	40%
Between Plan and 2 pct. points under Plan	30%
More than 2 pct. points under Plan	0%

The use of profit modifiers is contingent, of course, on the willingness of management to report financial results to employees. If the company is not willing to divulge this information, a variable share based on profitability should not even be considered.

More recently, variable shares or modifiers based on variables other than profitability have been emerging. The air conditioner manufacturer program outlined in Chapter 8 provided an example of a modifier based on quality, while the Control Data plan also uses a modifier based on the results of a customer survey.

In general, a modifier allows the modifying variable to have greater impact on employee bonuses than if it were simply one element of a family of measures. As a modifier, it can substantially change, or even eliminate, the employee share of the bonus pool. It is for this reason that the variables used as modifiers generally represent superordinate goals, such as quality, customer satisfaction, and profitability.

The Payout Frequency

The next logical design component is the Payout Frequency. How often should gains be paid to employees?

There is a significant trade-off to be considered here. On the one hand it is a good idea to pay bonuses frequently so that the reward follows closely behind the behaviors that generated the gains. Experiments in behavior modification have shown that prompt and frequent reinforcement for a desired behavior will more quickly condition an individual to adopt that behavior on a routine basis. If a company wants employees to become more involved in improving organizational performance then, it should reward them as soon as possible after they do so. It might well conclude that payouts should be made on a weekly basis, or at least no less frequently than monthly.

But the value of the reinforcement as well as its frequency should also be considered. An inconsequential reward may not be effective in shaping behavior no matter how frequently it is administered. The more frequent the gain sharing payout, the smaller its magnitude, all other things being equal; a company may therefore be diluting the effectiveness of the reward by very frequent payouts. This line of thinking would lead to less frequent payouts, such as quarterly, semi-annually or even annually. The cash profit sharing plan of the Anderson Group, maker of Anderson Windows, made national news in 1988 when it distributed an annual payout to its employees of $28,000 per person. The payout wasn't frequent, but you can bet it got their employees' attention!

Most plans, with the exception of profit sharing, pay bonuses on a monthly or quarterly basis. Either of these options probably represent a reasonable balance between the need for frequent reinforcement and the need for meaningful payout amounts. Profit sharing, of course, has traditionally been associated with annual payouts, although this is changing. Motorola, for example, uses a semi-annual payout in their program (Chapter 7).

The availability of formula data limits the options for the frequency decision. For this reason, weekly payouts are virtually always limited to physical productivity plans, such as IMPRO-SHARE®. Financial, cost, or profitability data are simply not available in many organizations except on a monthly basis.

Another consideration is the volatility of the formula. Consider the chart in Figure 10-1. The gain sharing formula fluctuates dramatically from month to month; one month there is a substantial gain, and in the next month there is a substantial loss. Over the course of the year, the gains and the losses in this scenario basically wash each other out and no net gain results. Had this plan been structured around a monthly payout, however, the company would have paid bonuses in several of the months. While the employees would be happy to accept the additional compensation, this is certainly not a desirable outcome from the company's point of view. One solution to this problem is a less frequent payout, perhaps quarterly or semi-annually. The short-term gains would then be offset by subsequent losses, and payouts would be reduced or eliminated. This is not the only solution to the volatility problem; as Chapter 11 will explain, there are several options that reduce the volatility risk while allowing for more frequent payouts.

Some managers would argue that less frequent payouts are desirable in order to protect employees from themselves. An extended period of substantial weekly bonuses might tempt employees to adjust their standard of living by taking on additional debt to finance a bigger house, a bigger car, or any number of other luxuries. But variable compensation can go down as well as up, and the imprudent employee might find himself in difficult financial straits should the bonus decline or disappear for an extended period of time. If bonuses are paid only a few times a year, on the other hand, it is less likely that employees will rely on them to pay for the groceries or make the mortgage payment.

A final consideration for the frequency component is administrative cost. There are certainly costs associated with gain sharing payouts—checks must be cut and payroll records must be updated. Less frequent payouts, accordingly, would minimize these administrative costs. This criterion should not normally be the deciding factor in the frequency decision, however. If a plan is inordinately costly to administer, its design should be reconsidered.

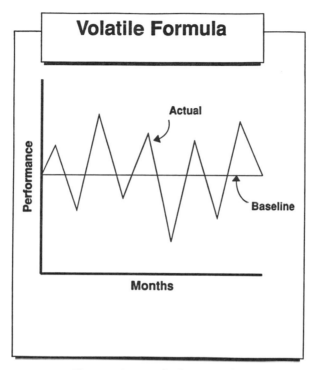

Figure 10-1. Volatile Formula.

Payout Frequency Variations

As with the other design components, there are non-standard or unusual features with respect to payout frequency as well.

A restaurant chain, for example, used a *dual frequency* in its pilot gain sharing programs.[1] In this case, hourly employees were paid bonuses on a monthly basis, while managers received quarterly payouts. This feature presumably ensured that managers would adopt a longer-term outlook in their decision making.

Another non-traditional feature is the *variable payout frequency*. In plans with variable frequencies, there is no fixed payout schedule. Instead, the gain sharing pool accumulates over time until it reaches a predetermined level ($50,000 for example), at which time it is paid out. The primary attraction of the variable frequency is that it ensures that payouts are made only when the amount of money involved is substantial.

There are no rules, of course, requiring that the payout frequency conform to the standard calendar format. Payouts at Atwood Industries, the company with the 36-year Scanlon Plan, coincide with the company's thirteen four-week accounting periods. And the Chrysler Acustar plan at Dayton (Chapter 7) pays out in July and December, thus resulting in one five-month and one seven-month gain sharing period each year.

The Split

The last of the required design components is perhaps the most controversial. The Split refers to the method of distribution of the employee share of the bonus pool, or how the employee share is divided among the individual employees. No other design component seems to cause controversy and conflict to the degree that this one does. To make matters worse, there are legal restrictions on the option that is often the most palatable to those involved.

There are three basic options for this component, with a number of variants as well. The three basic options are summarized in Table 10-3.

Table 10–3

Split Options

Option 1: Percent of Income

$$\frac{\$\,Pool}{\$\,Payroll} = \%$$

Option 2: Equal Shares

$$\frac{\$\,Pool}{\#\,Employees} = \$/Employee$$

Option 3: Hours Worked

$$\frac{\$\,Pool}{Hours\,Worked} = \$/Hour$$

In the percent-of-income method, the employee share of the pool is divided by the participating payroll cost in order to obtain a percentage. The amount of bonus received by each employee is the resulting percentage multiplied by his total pay for the period (as will be explained later, applying this to only his base pay does not meet legal requirements).

The principal argument for this option is that it maintains the integrity of the pay system. Presumably, differentials in pay reflect variations in level of contribution to the success of the business (the word *presumably* should be emphasized, as this is not always the case). And if indeed the higher-paid employees make a greater contribution, one could argue that they should receive a larger bonus than the lower-paid employees. The percent-of-income method accomplishes this; the higher the pay, the higher the bonus. The survey mentioned earlier on non-traditional rewards indicated that this is the most common option, in use in 50% of the responding firms.[2] Its leading position among the three options may also reflect its use in the standardized plans—Scanlon, Rucker®, and IMPROSHARE®.

Gain sharing design teams, however, often find reason to reject the percent-of-income approach. Hourly employees, who are producing the product or service and have direct impact on the measures, may not feel that it is fair that salaried staff employees receiver higher bonuses than they do. In addition, gain sharing is a team bonus, and differentials in payouts among individuals may undermine the team spirit. Furthermore, even if one accepts the premise that base pay differentials reflect individual contribution, it would take a great leap of faith to accept that base pay differentials reflect *team* contribution. Some of the highest-paid people, in fact, could possibly be the worst team players, and vice versa.

After much discussion and deliberation, design teams often reach consensus around the second distribution option, equal shares. Here the pool is simply divided by the number of participating employees, with every employee receiving the same dollar bonus. This approach seems to appeal to employees' sense of fairness and equity and (not surprisingly) is particularly favored by the lower-paid employees.

The equal-shares option is the second most prevalent choice (used by 17% of the companies surveyed). Its use would probably be considerably greater except for one unfortunate circumstance: it violates federal law! The law in question is the Fair Labor Standards Act (FLSA), which, among other things, requires that non-exempt employees be paid a 50% premium over their base rate for all hours worked in excess of 40 per week.

The FLSA states that all compensation must be considered when calculating the 50% premium, with only certain specific types of bonuses excepted:

◇ Gifts, such as Christmas turkeys.
◇ Discretionary bonuses.
◇ Bonuses relating to a bona fida profit-sharing plan or trust.

Obviously, gain sharing programs (other than profit sharing) do not qualify as one of the enumerated exceptions. This is reinforced further by wording in the Code of Federal Regulations relative to profit-sharing plans. A plan is not deemed to be a bona fide profit-sharing plan, "if the share of any individual employee is determined in substance on the basis of attendance, quality or quantity of work, rate of production, or efficiency.[3]

Our first option, distribution by percent of income, meets the legal test because overtime pay is included in the denominator when calculating the payout percentage. The employee who works overtime will therefore receive a bonus that reflects the 50% premium that is required by law. For this reason, the percent-of-income method on base pay alone is not acceptable in the eyes of the law.

The equal-shares approach, with no other adjustments, fails to meet FLSA requirements because all employees receive the same bonus, regardless of overtime worked. Equal shares is feasible from a legal standpoint only if management *retroactively adjusts overtime pay*. In other words, the bonus must be added to the employee's base pay for the period and the 50% premium rate recalculated on that basis. Because this overtime rate will be higher than that used in originally compensating the employee for overtime hours, a company must pay the difference to all non-exempt employees who worked overtime in the period covered by the bonus. Few companies, of course, want to do this.

Interestingly enough, equal-share plans are not hard to find, in spite of their illegal status. Only a handful of companies—Xerox is one example—make the retroactive adjustment required to legitimize them. Invariably, the existence of these plans simply reflects ignorance of the law rather than an intentional flouting of the law.

As awareness of the legal problems associated with equal shares has grown in recent years, the third distribution option has become more prevalent. In this option, the employee share of the pool is divided by the total hours worked (or paid) by participating employees in order to obtain a dollars-per-hour bonus payment. Equal-share proponents generally find this method to be preferable to the percent-of-income option, because it is not impacted by differentials in base pay rates. Some even prefer it to equal shares on the basis that the employee who works more hours deserves a larger piece of the pool.

In order to be legal with the hours-worked distribution approach, a company does have to adopt one convention—it must count the equivalent overtime premium hours for non-exempt employees. In other words, overtime hours must be treated as 1½ hours, both in calculating the bonus rate per hour and in applying it to the individuals involved. It should be noted that this distribution method is not specifically sanctioned by the law; however, it clearly complies with the intent of the law.

The principle problem with the hours-worked approach lies in the treatment of exempt or salaried employees. Most companies do not keep track of the hours worked for these employees (and don't want to). The logical solution, of course is to credit all salaried employees, for bonus distribution purposes, with the normal work hours, for example, 40 hours per week. But now another inequity is created, for many of these employees do work additional hours. Under the percent-of-income method, these employees received the highest bonus; now they receive the lowest. Should one inequity be solved by creating another?

About the only solution to this dilemma is to credit all exempt employees with something greater than the number of regular work hours. Plans that credit salaried employees with 42 or 45 hours (or even more) are not uncommon.

Hybrid Distribution Methods

In their zeal to resolve this Split issue in a way that more closely approximates equal shares, gain sharing design teams have come up with some distribution methods that represent interesting variations on the three basic methods.

One of these involves using multiple percentages in a percent-of-income distribution. The FLSA does allow for different percentages to be used for different categories of employees, such as those based on length of service. Thus lower-paid job classes could presumably be awarded a higher-percentage bonus than the high-paid classes, thus leveling out somewhat the differences in absolute-dollar bonuses paid.

Another variant is the *segmented pool.* In one example of this approach, the bonus pool is divided into two separate pools, one for exempt employees and one for non-exempt employees. The basis for the separation is the number of participating employees in each group. If 20% of the participating employees are exempt, for example, the exempt pool would represent 20% of the total. The non-exempt pool is then distributed on the basis of percent of income, thus complying with the law. The exempt pool, however, is distributed in equal shares (or any other method). The effect of this is that *on average,* exempt and non-exempt employees receive equal amounts.

Yet another innovation is that adopted by Eggers Industries in their Multi-Cost Ratio plan (Chapter 7). The percent-of-income method is used here, with an added provision: no salaried employee can receive a larger bonus than the highest one paid to an hourly employee. This puts a cap on individual payouts and thus reduces the range of bonus payments.

As one might expect, the law is somewhat complex, and anyone considering a creative alternative with regard to the distribution method would be well advised to obtain a legal opinion as to its legitimacy.

Summary

The final required design components are the Share, the Frequency, and the Split. As with the other components, these features must be clearly defined as integral elements of the gain sharing plan.

The Share refers to the proportion of the gains that will be paid out to participating employees. The most common approach is a simple 50/50 division between the company and employees. While this option benefits from an inherent sense of equity, it is not necessarily the best choice. Factors that should be considered in reaching a decision on this component include the nature of the formula, the capital intensity of the business, and decisions made around the baseline.

Consideration of the Payout Frequency basically involves the evaluation of a trade-off: frequency versus magnitude of reinforcement. Other criteria include data availability, formula variability, and administrative cost. The majority of gain sharing plans use either monthly or quarterly payouts.

The Split is often a controversial issue because it determines how the employee share of the bonus pool will be distributed to individual participants. Basic options include percent of income, equal shares, and hours worked. The decision is complicated by legal requirements, which limit the ability to use the equal-share option. There are, however, variations on the percent-of-income approach that can serve to lessen the differentials among payments to individuals.

References

1. Jewell, Donald O. and Jewell, Sandra F., "An Example of Economic Gainsharing in the Restaurant Industry." *National Productivity Review,* Spring, 1987.
2. O'Dell, Carla and McAdams, Jerry, *People, Performance, and Pay.* Houston, TX: American Productivity and Quality Center, 1987.
3. "Regulations, Part 549: Bona-Fide Profit-Sharing Plan or Trust Under the Fair Labor Standards Act." Washington, DC: U.S. Department of Labor, Employment Standards Administration, Wage and Hour Division, 1980.

Chapter 11

Optional
Design Components

Chapters 3 through 10 reviewed the basic design components, along with the options for each, of a gain sharing system. Once design decisions have been made around these components, the structure for a viable, launchable system is in place.

Before the button is pushed, however, some additional design features should be considered. While these features are not required for a workable gain sharing program, they may make a great deal of sense in some circumstances. In certain situations, in fact, they may be critical to the long-term viability of the system. The design process is really not complete until review of the need for these optional components is made.

The three most common of the optional components are:

◇ Smoothing mechanisms
◇ Caps and buy-backs
◇ Capital investment adjustments

Each of these optional design components will now be reviewed for its rationale and the mechanics of integrating it into the gain sharing system. As with the required components, there are generally several options available for dealing with each.

Smoothing Mechanisms

A smoothing mechanism is a design component that is often over-looked by gain sharing designers. This is unfortunate, as it can be critically important to the viability of the program. The lack of this feature can even doom the system under certain circumstances.

Basically, the purpose of a smoothing mechanism is to level out the inherent variability in the gain sharing measures. Rarely does improvement take place in a smooth, unbroken fashion. More likely, periodic setbacks will occur which will temporarily interrupt the upward trend.

Why is this relevant to the design of a gain sharing system? Table 11-1 shows some simple hypothetical examples.

Table 11–1

Effect of Variability

	QUARTER				Full
	1	2	3	4	Year
Example A					
Gain	$100	$100	$(100)	$100	$200
Employee Share (50%)	50	50	-	50	150
Example B					
Gain	$100	$100	$(200)	$100	$100
Employee Share (50%)	50	50	-	50	150
Example C					
Gain	$100	$100	$(400)	$100	$(100)
Employee Share (50%)	50	50	-	50	150

The scenario involves a quarterly payout. In Example A, the gains, as measured by the gain sharing formula, amount to $100 in the first, second, and fourth quarters. In the third quarter, however, there is a deficit of $100. The company's performance, in other words, failed to surpass the baseline during that period. If the four quarterly results are added up, they show a gain for the full year of $200. Fair enough; a gain was achieved even if it was somewhat uneven. Everyone has a bad quarter now and then.

But look at the payout to employees, which was assumed to be 50% of the gain. In three of the quarters, the company paid out $50; in the deficit quarter, of course, there was nothing to pay. Again adding up the quarters, the company paid out \$150, or 75% of the full-year gain. What happened to the company's 50% share?

Example B shows an even worse situation. Here the deficit has doubled in the third quarter, resulting in a full year gain of \$100. At least the company still had a positive year on balance. But it still paid out \$150, which was more than the gain itself! You can hear the wails coming from the executive offices: "I thought this was supposed to gain *sharing.*"

To see a real disaster, look at Example C. The company did well for three quarters, but got demolished in one. The damage was so bad that it had a net loss in the gain sharing plan for the year. But it still increased compensation. Is this supposed to improve its competitiveness?

Obviously, management will not live with a plan in which one of these scenarios is a recurring event. You can bet the program will be terminated. It doesn't do employees much good either; mixing increased pay with declining performance doesn't do much for job security.

This phenomenon is the outcome of a simple fact of gain sharing life: the company shares the gains, but it does not share the losses. It is hard to envision a program where employees write the company checks for their share of the deficits.

The implication of this phenomenon is clear: if even a single deficit period occurs during the course of a year, the employee share of the full-year gain will exceed the nominal share built into the plan.

The likelihood of this occurring can be lessened considerably, or even eliminated, through the use of a smoothing mechanism. Whether or not a smoothing mechanism is needed is dependent upon two things: the variability of the formula and the frequency of the payout. The greater the variability or volatility of the formula, the greater the potential of large gains offset by large deficits. And the more frequent the payout, the greater the likelihood that one or more deficits will occur over the course of a year.

A smoothing mechanism is a complication for the gain sharing plan, and most of the options have some negatives associated with them. If it is not needed, it should not be used. But if it is needed, it should not be avoided, as it can mean the difference between long-term success and failure.

Five different smoothing options are:

◇ Infrequent payout
◇ Deficit reserve

◇ Rolling payout
◇ Loss recovery
◇ Year-to-date payout

Infrequent Payout

The simplest approach to reduce volatility is to pay bonuses less frequently, such as semi-annually or annually. It may be recalled from the discussion of Payout Frequency (Chapter 10) that formula variability was one of the criteria for making this decision. With this option, short-term gains and losses will be offset against each other, thus reducing the risk of overpaying the gain.

The major drawback of the infrequent payout is the loss of frequent reinforcement for improvement. It may also be recalled from the Payout Frequency discussion that regular and frequent reinforcement is an important factor in changing people's behavior. With an annual payout particularly, there should be concern about maintaining the visibility of and enthusiasm for the gain sharing program.

Deficit Reserve

The most common response to the variability problem is the deficit reserve; its frequency of use probably exceeds all of the other options put together. It should not be construed from this fact, however, that the deficit reserve is the best choice for smoothing out formula variability. Actually, it is probably the most complicated of the options and may at the same time be the least effective. In addition, its purpose is often misunderstood. Its popularity is simply a matter of tradition—it is a feature of the Scanlon Plan and thus has a long history of use. Many students of gain sharing are not even aware that there are other options for reducing variability.

In a plan with a deficit reserve, a predetermined percentage of the employee share is withheld each period and placed in a reserve account. This percentage ranges anywhere from 10% to 50%, with 25% being the most common. This withholding continues for each period in which there is a payout, with the withheld amounts accumulating in the reserve account. The deficit reserve serves its purpose in a period where there is a negative gain, or deficit. When this occurs, the employee share of the deficit is charged to the reserve account, thus reducing its positive balance. In effect, the company has recovered some of the employee share from earlier (or later) periods.

Using the same data from our hypothetical Example A in Table 11-1, the workings of a 20% deficit reserve can be seen in Table 11-2.

Table 11–2
Mechanics of Deficit Reserve

| | QUARTER | | | | Full |
	1	2	3	4	Year
Gain	$100	$100	$(100)	$100	$200
Employee Share (50%)	50	50	-	50	150
Withheld for Reserve (20%)	10	10	-	10	30
Paid out	$40	$40	-	$40	$120
Reserve Balance	$10	$20	$(30)*	$(20)	

*50% of the deficit is charged against the reserve.

In the example, the company paid out $120 instead of $150 over the course of the year. It still paid more than the intended 50% of the gains, so the deficit reserve did not totally solve its problem. But it did reduce the damage. Had the company wanted greater protection, of course, it could have withheld a higher percentage of the employee share.

In most cases, the deficit reserve is zeroed out at year-end. If there is a positive balance, it is paid out to employees; it is their money and the company did not need it to offset deficits. If the account carries a negative balance, it is absorbed by the company.

A few gain sharing plans use a continuous accrual form of the deficit reserve. Any negative balance is not zeroed out at year-end, but carries over into the next year. This assures that deficits will ultimately be recovered (assuming the plan has sufficient payouts in the future to do so). With the continuous accrual approach, some decision rule to pay out all or part of the reserve is needed if a positive balance continues to grow.

There are two major disadvantages to the deficit reserve: it is somewhat complicated and employees tend to have negative feelings about it. Some will contend employees should get their full share when they earned it. Others will ask why there is nothing reserved from the company share. These attitudes tend to reflect a lack of understanding of the purpose of the deficit reserve, and may be offset by an effective education strategy.

The deficit reserve is often confused with another feature that is sometimes found in gain sharing plans. A portion of the employee share may be withheld and accumulated in a reserve account for the purpose of paying bonuses in periods in which no gains have been realized. The objective here is to avoid a loss of enthusiasm by ensuring that employees receive bonuses even during temporary slack periods. Because the company cannot ever recover any of this money, this technique has absolutely nothing to do with reducing the variability risk to the company.

Rolling Payout

The next most common mechanism, after the deficit reserve, is the rolling payout. This is not to be confused with the rolling baseline, which was discussed in Chapter 9.

In the rolling payout approach, bonuses are based on the *average* performance of two or more periods rather than on that of a single period. A two-quarter rolling payout, for example, would share with employees the average gains of the previous two quarters; a three-month rolling payout would base payouts on the average gain of the previous three months. Using the earlier example, the impact of a two-quarter rolling payout is presented in Table 11-3. This approach, given the hypothetical data, brought the employee share back to where it was intended to be. Had there been a larger deficit in the third quarter, however, it would have been only partially effective.

Table 11–3
Mechanics of Two-Quarter Rolling Payout

| | QUARTER | | | | Full |
	1	2	3	4	Year
Gain	$100	$100	$(100)	$100	$200
Average Two-Quarter Gain	100*	100	0	0	
Employee Share (50%)	50	50	-	-	100

*Assumes that the gain in the fourth quarter of the prior year was $100.

The rolling payout does totally eliminate the variability problem if it is carried far enough. A quarterly plan with a four-quarter rolling payout (or a monthly plan with a twelve-month rolling payout) carries no risk of paying out a larger-than-intended employee share over the course of a year.

The IMPROSHARE® plan uses a rolling payout in that bonuses are typically based on a four-week rolling average. The 3M company (Chapter 6) provides one example of a four-quarter rolling average payout.

The major objection to the rolling payout option is that it dilutes the psychological impact of both good and bad performance periods. If employees really get it together and achieve extraordinary gains in a given period, the reinforcement (in the form of gain sharing bonuses) will be muted because this performance will be averaged with the previous period. By the same token, negative reinforcement for poor performance will be ameliorated if a bonus is earned anyway because of the effect of a prior period's gain.

Loss Recovery

Of more recent vintage than the other smoothing alternatives discussed thus far is the Loss Recovery method. In this approach, the employees' share of the gains is reduced (or eliminated) in periods following the occurrence of a deficit until that deficit has been recovered by the company.

Table 11-4 presents an example of the Loss Recovery method. This example assumes that the employee share is reduced by half following a deficit period.

With the hypothetical numbers used in the example, this method only partially recovered the deficit for the year. However, the loss recovery adjustment to the employee share would normally continue into the following year. It could thus be expected to be more effective than the deficit reserve, which is usually terminated at year-end.

How long the loss recovery adjustment continues after a deficit varies from program to program. In some cases, the reduced employee share continues until the deficit has been recovered, no matter how long it takes. In other cases, a time limit is set (typically four quarters) to ensure that a large deficit does not affect the payout for years to come.

There are systems in which the employee share is eliminated entirely following a deficit period. While this certainly speeds the

Table 11–4

Mechanics of 50% Loss Recovery

| | QUARTER | | | | Full |
	1	2	3	4	Year
Gain	$100	$100	$(100)	$100	$200
Employee Share before Loss Recovery (50%)	50	50	-	50	150
Employee Share after Loss Recovery (25%)	50	50	-	25	125
Amount Remaining to be Recovered	-	-	(50)	(25)	

recovery of the deficit for the company, one should be concerned about the potential for a highly detrimental impact on the motivation to improve in future periods.

Year-to-date Payout

The final method for smoothing formula variability is the year-to-date payout. The idea here is that the cumulative payout during the course of the year should never exceed the employee share of the year-to-date gains. To obtain the payout for a given period, the employee share of the year-to-date gains is calculated and then the total amount paid out so far during the year is subtracted. If the balance is positive, that is the amount paid.

As the example in Table 11-5 shows, this approach ensured that the company did not pay bonuses in the fourth quarter and thus maintained the full-year integrity of the system. Different numbers, of course, would not necessarily give the same result.

The principle drawback of the year-to-date payout is that its effectiveness in dealing with deficits diminishes as the year progresses. The earlier a deficit occurs in the year, the more time a company has to generate gains to offset that deficit. Unlike the other smoothing mechanisms, this method is totally useless in dealing with deficits that occur in the final period of the year.

Table 11–5
Mechanics of Year-to-Date Payout

| | QUARTER | | | | Full |
	1	2	3	4	Year
Gain	$100	$100	$(100)	$100	$200
Year-to-date Gain	$100	$200	$100	$200	
Employee Share of Year-to-Date Gain (50%)	50	100	50	100	
Payout	50	50	-	-	100

Caps and Buybacks

A question that management invariably raises when contemplating gain sharing is, "Should we have a cap on the payout?" This question is usually motivated by a fear that the gain sharing program will somehow "run away" and pay out too much money to participating employees.

It will be recalled from Chapter 1 that gain sharing should normally be self-funding. That is, the additional compensation is funded by the incremental gains that occur. If the system is carefully designed to ensure that self-funding occurs, this fear should, at least in theory, be unfounded. By definition, overpayment cannot occur in a self-funding system.

The biggest argument against caps is that they keep the gain sharing program from doing its job. If the company is truly receiving its fair share of the gains, why would it want to limit the amount of improvement that will be rewarded?

Nonetheless, management may be nervous about this non-traditional approach to rewards, and a cap may provide the comfort level necessary to gain approval from the decision makers. It is always possible, after all, that something may be overlooked in the design process that will undermine the self-funding nature of the system.

Actually, there is one argument for a payout cap that may have merit. Some would argue that there should be limits on the proportion of an employee's pay that is variable. The contention is that a high percentage of pay should be fixed so that employees can rely on a predictable level of income to manage their financial affairs. If their income is subject to wide swings, it may be difficult to make judicious decisions around expenditures and debt acquisition. A cap, of course, serves to ensure that bonuses will not become a dominant element of the employee's total compensation.

A cap, however, is not the only means of keeping bonuses from becoming very large; a rolling or ratcheting baseline (Chapter 9) will probably serve the same purpose. It is unlikely that extraordinarily large bonuses will be earned in a gain sharing program with an ever-tightening baseline.

The argument for a cap, therefore, becomes more compelling in a fixed-baseline gain sharing program. Assuming a company is successful in achieving continuous improvement, bonuses in such a system could be expected to grow over time, perhaps becoming quite large relative to base pay. A cap could be used in this case to trigger an adjustment to the baseline and bring bonuses back in line.

The IMPROSHARE® program (Chapter 6) epitomizes the use of a cap for this purpose. Bonuses under IMPROSHARE® are capped at 30% of pay (given the 50% share, this requires a 60% productivity improvement). If the 30% cap is exceeded in a given period, the excess is not forfeited by employees, but is set aside in a deferral account. This should not be confused with a deficit reserve; the money in the deferral account unconditionally belongs to employees and will be paid out ultimately. Payments are made out of the deferral account in subsequent periods when the payout is less than 30%. The deferral account thus serves to redistribute bonuses in excess of the cap to later periods when bonuses are lower.

When payouts consistently exceed the cap for an extended period, however, it is time to adjust the baseline (remember that standards in IMPROSHARE® are frozen and thus have not changed up to this point). As a practical matter, a company has to do something to get the bonus under the cap or it will not be able to draw down its deferral account, which has been growing ever larger.

The mechanism for making the adjustment is the *buyback*. The standards are tightened by an amount that will bring the current level of performance below the 30% cap. If, for example, a company wished to reduce the bonus from 30% to 20%, it would multiply each of the standards by the following factor:

$$\frac{140}{160} = .875$$

This adjustment would bring the current level of performance from 160% (a 30% bonus) of the baseline to 140% of the baseline (a 20% bonus). A company can also, if it wishes to, adjust the base productivity factor rather than (or in addition to) the standards.

In making this adjustment, however, the company has violated the fixed baseline feature of IMPROSHARE®, and it should compensate employees for this change. This is accomplished through a lump sum payment equal to one year's worth of the bonus that employees are losing as a result of this one-time baseline tightening.

Clearly, a cap should not be imposed on the gain sharing program without careful consideration. If the purpose of a cap if simply to limit the company's exposure, it will contribute nothing to the effective functioning of the gain sharing system. On the contrary, it may well prove to be a detriment, for at the same time it is limiting the company's exposure, it is also limiting the improvement potential. If, on the other hand, a cap is used to prevent variable pay from becoming too large a component of total compensation, management probably needs to incorporate the complications of deferral accounts and buybacks in order to keep the cap from having a dampening effect on the motivation to improve.

Capital Investment Adjustments

The third of the optional design features is adjustments for gains associated with capital investments. Any organization that makes, or is contemplating making, capital investments for the purpose of improving productivity or lowering costs would be well-advised to consider this feature.

In theory, adjustments to the plan should be made for any capital investment that improves the gain sharing formula. The nature of that adjustment would be to remove the capital-related gain from the pool that is to be shared with employees.

Capital investments, at least those that are designed to improve business performance, are made with the expectation that the company will realize a certain return on that investment. The source of funds for the investment is either borrowed money, in which case interest costs are incurred, or shareholders' equity, which involves an opportunity cost. If the investment cannot provide a return in excess of these costs (probably well in excess, in view of the risks associated with many types of capital investment), it should not be made.

If the gains from capital investments are allowed to flow into the bonus pool, where they will be shared with employees, the return to the company will obviously be reduced. Some investments, as a result, will no longer provide a return sufficient to justify the investment in the first place. Thus capital investments that are important to maintaining or improving the competitiveness of the business may not be made. An organization should not allow gain sharing to impede needed business investment.

Having recognized the need for capital investment adjustments, one should also recognize the downside: they complicate the gain sharing plan greatly. The calculations underlying the quantification of the gain are generally complicated; even professionals may not understand them. And constant adjustments to the plan are not desirable from a credibility standpoint. Employees will never be sure what numbers they are working against, and trust may suffer.

In view of the problems associated with capital investment adjustments, these adjustments probably should be minimized. This is normally done by adopting a plan provision that provides for adjustments only when *major* capital investments are made. What constitutes a major investment will, of course, vary from company to company. A $10,000 investment might be major for a small company, while $1 million or more might be a more appropriate threshold for a large, capital intensive, continuous process facility. In any event, the dollar limit should be defined by the plan so there are no misunderstandings on this point.

Certain plan features may ameliorate the capital investment problem considerably. Primary among these is a ratcheting or rolling baseline (Chapter 9). With a baseline that routinely repositions itself, capital investment adjustments are made *automatically*. When a normal and routine resetting of the baseline takes place, the gain associated with any prior capital investment will be part of the actual performance data, and the baseline will be tightened accordingly. Management may be comfortable in this circumstance with foregoing any special adjustment. The only concern may be with the length of time required for the baseline to fully adjust for the capital investment; with a three-year rolling baseline, for example, the capital-related gains will be shared (at least partially) for three years. Whether the movement of the baseline is adequate to deal with capital investments therefore is a judgmental decision.

Multi-cost ratios (Chapter 7) also offer an opportunity to limit or eliminate capital investment adjustments. This is done by including depreciation as one of the measured costs. Because capital investments result in increased depreciation costs, at least part of the gain will therefore be offset by higher depreciation. In spite of this benefit, the inclusion of depreciation costs in gain sharing programs is rather uncommon because the accounting is difficult to explain and it is uncontrollable by most employees.

If, all things having been considered, it is deemed necessary to allow for capital investment adjustments, the plan designers must then determine the method and timing of the adjustments.

The usual method is the *full adjustment.* The effect of the capital investment on the gain sharing formula is calculated and the baseline is tightened by that amount. Because the actual performance and the baseline have both changed by the same amount, there is (at least theoretically) no effect on the gain that is being shared. A highly simplified example of the full-adjustment approach is presented in Table 11-6.

Table 11-6
Full Capital Investment Adjustment

	Before Adjustment	After Adjustment
Formula Value	120	125
Baseline	100	105
Gain	20	20

*Note: Assumes the capital investment improves the formula by 5.

Prior to the capital investment, the actual value of the gain sharing measure was 120. Compared to a baseline of 100, the company was enjoying (and sharing) a gain of 20. A capital investment then improved its measure from 120 to 125. In order to eliminate this gain from the sharing process, the company must increase the baseline by the same amount, from 100 to 105. Employees have lost nothing, as the gain remains at 20.

Another adjustment method is the *partial adjustment.* A feature of IMPROSHARE® and the 3M Company plans, among others, this approach adjusts the baseline by less than (80% is typical) the full amount of the capital-related gain. This method is depicted in Table 11-7.

Table 11-7
Partial Capital Investment Adjustment

	Before Adjustment	After Adjustment
Formula Value	120	125
Baseline	100	104
Gain	20	21

*Note: Assumes the capital investment improves the formula by 5, and the baseline adjustment is 80%.

Here is the same situation as in the previous example: the capital investment has improved the value of the measure from 120 to 125. But with an 80% adjustment, the increase in the baseline is limited to a value of 4. The gain to be shared therefore increases.

Why would a company make only a partial adjustment for capital investments? The reason is to motivate employees to support the company's capital investment programs. There are probably few investments whose full success is not dependent, at least in part, on the efforts of employees to make them work.

Under normal circumstances, these efforts may not be forthcoming, particularly because capital investments have traditionally been used to eliminate jobs. The partial adjustment mechanism, by sharing a portion of the gains from capital investments, should improve employee receptivity to and support for capital improvements.

As with everything else in gain sharing, there are variations on the basic approaches. One of these is the *share-after-payback* option. This approach involves a full baseline adjustment, followed by a reversion of the baseline to an unadjusted state after the payback has been achieved. This method probably only makes sense in a fixed-baseline program.

Guidelines regarding the timing of capital investment adjustments should also be established. Rarely does a major piece of capital equipment go into place smoothly, instantaneously producing the anticipated gains. More likely, there will be a period of disruption, accompanied by higher costs, and a gradual climb to normal productive use and a full realization of the intended improvements.

Under these circumstances, an immediate adjustment to the baseline to reflect the anticipated gains would be unfair to the plan participants. Not only have the gains not yet occurred, but there may even be a decline in performance as a result of the disruptions and added costs associated with the installation of the new equipment.

There should, accordingly, be a lag between the time of installation of the capital equipment and the baseline adjustment. The adjustment could, of course, simply be delayed until the equipment has reached its peak operating status. This, of course, requires a judgment call.

Another solution is to specify a consistent, predetermined lag for all capital-related adjustments. For example, the plan may require that baseline adjustments be made three months following the installation of the new equipment. In addition to removing the judgment factor, this option offers another potential benefit. Employees may be more motivated to support and accelerate the installation process, for they will fully share in the gains generated by the capital investment up until the point that the adjustment is made.

Whatever options are selected for handling capital investments, it is important that these provisions by spelled out in advance. If expectations for capital investment adjustments are not established, employees may feel they are being manipulated when they occur.

Summary

There are several gain sharing design features that, while not absolutely necessary for the implementation of a functional gain sharing program, can enhance the viability and equity of the system under certain circumstances. As such, their use should be considered by those charged with designing the plan.

A smoothing mechanism will probably be needed to protect the company from overpaying where the formula is volatile or the payout is relatively frequent. A cap on the bonus may be needed in a fixed-baseline gain sharing program in order to keep the variable component of compensation from becoming too large relative to fixed pay. Finally, capital investment adjustments should be provided for where potential capital investments are significant, unless automatic baseline movements are adequate to ensure that the returns are not unduly diluted.

As with the required gain sharing components, there are various alternative approaches for each of these optional features. Selection from among these options should be made based on consideration of the circumstances, business requirements, and the need for equity.

Chapter 12

Related Issues

The preceding eight chapters reviewed in some detail the major gain sharing design components. Beyond the technical design of the system, there are several other issues that affect the administration of the program and the integration of gain sharing into the organization's compensation system. Depending on the circumstances, some or all of these issues must be explicitly addressed.

These non-design issues can be divided into several categories.

◇ Compensation issues
- Impact of gain sharing on base pay strategies
- Fit with individual incentives
◇ Administrative issues
- Eligibility—new hires, terminations, etc.
- Payment procedures
◇ Collective bargaining issues

Compensation Issues

Gain sharing, of course, will not be the only form of compensation in the organization. At a minimum, there will be a system of base pay as well. Merit or other types of increases will likely be associated with that base pay system. There may also be more traditional forms of incentive; piecework or small-group production incentives are still widespread in manufacturing industries today.

How does gain sharing integrate with these other forms of compensation? Does it substitute for increases in base pay? Does it replace piecework incentives? Can it be used to determine base pay increases? These are complex issues, and the answers will vary based on the situation.

Impact on Base Pay Strategies

Traditionally, American business organizations have sought to maintain base pay at levels that are competitive with those of similar industries in the surrounding geographic area. Barring financial difficulties, the base pay structure could normally be expected to increase on an annual basis.

With the installation of gain sharing, management is faced with an inevitable decision: will base pay continue to increase over time as it has in the past?

If the primary purpose of gain sharing is variable compensation, one could easily argue that base pay should not increase as it has in the past (at least not to the same degree it would if there were no variable compensation). An organization would want to pay employees more only when the business is doing well; when times are tough, total compensation should decline below competitive levels and thus provide the company with some cost relief. By limiting or eliminating future increases in base pay, a company would gradually reach the state where base pay is less than competitive levels, with variable pay making up the difference. This approach is known as "pay-at-risk" because employees would likely earn less in tough times than they would have had there been no gain sharing program.

The problem with this logic is that the company may have difficulty attracting and retaining people, particularly during the difficult periods when no bonuses are being paid. If an individual can earn competitive pay on a fixed basis at another company, why would he choose to work for an organization where his pay reaches competitive levels only during periods of high performance?

One possible answer, of course, is that the potential employee might be attracted by the possibility of earning *more* than a competitive pay when the organization performs. For this to occur, however, requires that the bonus potential be relatively large. While some companies have successfully pursued this strategy—most notably, Nucor Corporation, with its 100% bonuses—this approach conflicts directly with the desire of many companies to prevent variable pay from becoming too large a proportion of total compensation (Chapter 11).

Another problem with pay-at-risk was encountered by Du Pont's Fibers Division in 1990. Du Pont's plan received extensive press coverage when it was launched in 1989. The plan provided that division employees would receive smaller salary increases than their counterparts in other Du Pont divisions. Bonuses would be paid, however, when division profitability goals were met. If profitability was great enough, Fibers Division employees could more than recover their foregone raises and come out ahead.

The press coverage was also extensive when Du Pont terminated the program less than two years later. It seems that profitability in 1990 was not adequate to pay bonuses, and employees were dissatisfied over having given up fixed pay and getting nothing in return. The problem was exacerbated by the fact that bonuses were tied to profitability, which most employees felt was out of their control.

For these reasons, many companies have concluded that they will continue to maintain base pay at levels that are competitive in the area. Gain sharing bonuses would therefore be add-on compensation for performance over and above that expected for base pay. This decision appears to be particularly prevalent among large companies that are leaders in their industries; Xerox, Motorola, and the 3M Company are all examples.

The idea of gain sharing as an add-on becomes easier to accept if you view the system's primary purpose as supporting a participative management process. The company's pursuit of employee participation is predicated on the belief that a high-involvement culture will produce a significantly higher level of business performance. If this is in fact the outcome, should employees not be compensated at a level that reflects their greater contribution? The highest-performing company in its industry, if it expects to retain that lofty position, surely must compensate its employees at a level that *exceeds* the competitive benchmark.

Nonetheless, there are circumstances where management must use gain sharing as a substitute for increases in base pay. If the company is uncompetitive because its compensation costs are high relative to its competitors, it may have little choice but to make *any* increase in compensation contingent upon the achievement of higher levels of performance. Assuming that employees understand the company's predicament, gain sharing can serve to energize the organization to improve competitiveness and reward employees beyond what may have been possible otherwise.

The degree to which gain sharing leads to modification in base pay strategies, therefore, is dependent upon circumstances. The competitive enterprise that is seeking to take its performance to a higher plane through employee involvement could be expected to maintain a competitive base pay; to do otherwise would be to risk under compensating a high-performing organization. For the company that is uncompetitive because its compensation costs are out-of-line, on the other hand, it may be necessary to adopt the position that any future increases must be funded by performance improvement.

Fit With Individual Incentives

Piecework incentives have been a fixture in the manufacturing landscape for decades. They are designed to provide an incentive for employees to work at a fast pace in order to maximize output. They are probably, to at least some degree, successful in doing that.

For those companies that have these individual incentive plans and are considering gain sharing, some difficult questions arise. Should gain sharing replace the individual incentive? If so, how does management protect incentive employees from a drop in income, and what is the expected effect on productivity? Can gain sharing be paid in addition to an individual incentive?

If there is a trend in this arena, it is toward the elimination of piecework incentives. Many companies feel these systems fail to meet their business needs today for a variety of reasons:

◇ The business focus is changing. Piecework incentives may have made sense when productivity and labor costs were the main focus of improvement efforts. Today, however, companies are more likely to have established quality or customer satisfaction as the top organizational priority. Any incentive system that rewards quantity, rather than quality, may undermine management's exhortations to "Do it right the first time." By the same token, many companies are attempting to increase responsiveness to customers and reduce in-process inventories by producing in small lot sizes. This manufacturing philosophy surely conflicts with a produce-as-much-as-you-can mentality.

◇ Job design assumptions are changing. Chapter 2 pointed out that the Scientific Management principles of Frederick Taylor (specialization and simple, repetitive job tasks) are giving way to multi-skilled work teams. Piecework incentives make little sense where the job design is intended to promote job rotation, teamwork, problem solving, and greater employee involvement in business decisions.

◊ Piecework incentives are costly to maintain and often have been poorly maintained. Plants with traditional incentive systems may require a department full of industrial engineers just to keep the incentive standards up to date. Even so, this task has been neglected by many companies. As a result, these systems are often inaccurate, inequitable, and ineffective.

◊ Piecework systems may cause dissatisfaction and conflict. Traditional incentives invariably are limited in application to direct labor employees, or at least to those employees whose output can be quantified. This leaves a sizeable portion of the work force without incentives and therefore without a means to increase their income through their own efforts. It would not be surprising if these people felt disadvantaged, unfairly treated, and even resentful of their incentive-earning peers.

To many companies with traditional incentives, gain sharing appears to be an ideal solution to the problem, for it represents a replacement for the piecework system. The offending incentives can be eliminated, to be replaced by a system that rewards all employees for pursuing the current business priorities, be they quality, customer service, or cost.

While the logic of using gain sharing as a replacement for incentives may be appealing, this maneuver is by no means simple to execute. First of all, there are added costs associated with this approach, for a temporary decline in productivity is all but inevitable. If it is true that an individual incentive causes people to work harder, then it must also be true that the removal of an incentive will slow the work pace. Hopefully, the productivity decline will be temporary; non-incentive employees will probably increase their productivity under gain sharing, and the greater attention paid by all to other performance variables (quality, material utilization, etc.) should provide some offsetting gains. Even the employees with previously established incentives tend to gradually improve their productivity under gain sharing after the initial decline. But even a temporary decline can be painful, however, and it can be precipitous—a 25% productivity drop among incentive employees is not unheard of.

There is also the risk of alienating a large and important group of workers—those covered by the old incentive. Clearly, any loss of income is not likely to be well received, even with a potential for recovering this loss through gain sharing. The recovery surely will not be immediate (and may never occur for those with high incentive earnings). Furthermore, their variable pay will no longer be under their exclusive control with gain sharing, but will be dependent upon the actions of others as well. It is important, therefore, that the incentive employee's loss of income be minimized or eliminated.

The only likely solution that will be totally acceptable to all incentive employees is to permanently adjust their base pay by an amount equal to their past average incentive earnings. Their pay level will thus be maintained, and they won't have to work as hard for it. Unfortunately, this solution is usually the least desirable one from a company point of view, for obvious reasons. As a result, one of two other options are often considered:

◇ Temporary red circle. Under this option, incentive employees are guaranteed their average incentive pay, as above, but with limitations. They may receive this additional pay for one year, for example, or it may be gradually phased out over a period of years.

◇ Incentive buy-out. This approach involves the complete and immediate elimination of incentive pay, with all employees reverting to base pay alone. Incentive employees are compensated for this change, however, through a lump-sum payment. This payment is equal to the employee's average incentive earnings for a certain period of time, one year being typical. While this option has the advantage of immediately eliminating any discrepancies in pay, it does require a large, up-front payment by the company.

There is probably no solution to this problem that is going to satisfy all employees and the company as well. Because it directly and immediately affects the pay of a substantial number of employees, it can be one of the most difficult and emotional issues faced in the pursuit of a meaningful and effective gain sharing system. Nonetheless, many companies are stepping up to the challenge, for traditional incentives may represent a major inhibitor to achieving world-class status.

This is not to say, of course, that incentives *must* be eliminated if a gain sharing system is to be installed. A number of gain sharing companies have chosen to retain their piecework incentives, usually because management believes the incentive system is well maintained, effective, and not in conflict with business priorities. In these situations, the major issue revolves around whether or not incentive employees should be included in the gain sharing program.

While examples either way can be found, the argument for their inclusion is probably more compelling. Gain sharing is, after all, designed to promote employee involvement, teamwork, and a sense of shared objectives. Is there any less need of these things from incentive-earning employees? If the pay system, as it presently exists, is rational and equitable, does it make sense to offer potential pay increases to one group but not another?

The final concern that needs to be raised here is that gain sharing should not be approached simply as a vehicle to replace an outmoded incentive system. Pains have been taken earlier to establish the principle that gain sharing is associated with a certain management philosophy, a philosophy that represents change for most organizations. The *raison d'etre* for gain sharing ought to be to support cultural change, not to eliminate incentives. If incentive elimination is the sole motivation for gain sharing, the commitment and supporting processes will probably not be in place to make it work.

Administrative Issues

There are a few issues relative to the on-going administration of gain sharing that may seem relatively minor in the overall scheme of things. Failure to deal with these issues in advance, however, can turn them into irritants that consume more time to resolve than that required to deal with them in the first place. At worst, they could even undermine the credibility of the program.

These issues can be divided into two categories. Eligibility issues deal with the treatment of part-time and temporary employees, new hires, terminations, and leaves. Payment procedures address deductions, minimum payouts, and the payment vehicle.

Eligibility Issues

If an organization has, or may have, any temporary or part-time employees, the question of the eligibility of these employees must be answered.

Like many other aspects of gain sharing, there are no hard-and-fast rules governing this issue, and one can easily find examples of both the inclusion and exclusion of these employees. As a general observation, however, companies are more likely to include permanent, part-time employees in gain sharing programs than temporary workers.

In certain industries (retailing is a good example), part-time employees are significant in number and necessary to the operation of the business. These people are deemed to be as integral to the organization as their full-time peers; they just happen to work fewer hours. They perform a crucial function and may remain with the company for years. If this is the case, it may be hard to justify their exclusion from the gain sharing program.

Temporaries, on the other hand, are usually not viewed as true members of the organization. They are engaged to fill a short-term need, after which they sever their ties to the company.

A second eligibility issue relates to those employees who, for a variety of reasons, are not actively employed during the entire term of a gain sharing period. Some individuals may hire in during the period, and others will terminate their employment. Some may be on extended sick leave or disability. There may be absences from the work place for other legitimate reasons, such as jury duty or military leave. If a company wants to avoid controversy later, it must define how these circumstances will be handled.

Depending upon the choice of the method for distributing the bonus pool, there may be an automatic answer to the question, if the company is willing to accept it. Both the percent-of-income and the hours worked (or hours paid) methods (Chapter 10) prorate the bonus for any employee who has been on the active payroll for only a portion of the gain sharing period. The equal shares approach does not accomplish this proration, however, and unless specified otherwise, a new hire or termination who spent one day on the job would have to be awarded a full share.

Even where the automatic proration mechanism exists, however, it may be deemed undesirable to include certain categories of employees. A newly employed worker, for example, may contribute little to the measured gains; he may even be a detriment because of his inexperience. Many would argue that an employee who resigns during the bonus period should not be rewarded either.

A common plan feature to deal with these issues is a provision that provides that an employee must be on the active payroll on both the first day and last day of the payout period in order to be eligible for a bonus. Others will employ a waiting period; for example, an employee is eligible during the first full payout period following six months of employment.

Clearly, a failure to think through these eligibility issues can only lead to controversy later.

Payment Procedures

The first question that typically arises around payment proce- dures is whether or not the bonus should be paid in a separate check. Most plan designers conclude that it should. The gain sharing bonus is an extra reward for exemplary performance, and as such, should be paid in a form that gives it extra visibility and impact. If it were simply incorporated into the regular paycheck, it surely would not carry the same emphasis. In addition, paying by separate check probably makes it easier for the employee to separate the bonus from his regular pay, thus lessening somewhat the likelihood that plan participants will use variable pay for day-to-day living expenses.

Another payment issue concerns statutory deductions for income taxes and social security. The issue is not whether these deductions must be taken; there is no question that that is a legal requirement. The problem arises when participants are not informed in advance of these deductions. The excitement generated by an announcement of a $500 bonus payment turns to confusion, consternation, and even suspicions of manipulation when the actual check turns out to be only $400. It is a shame to allow such a letdown to occur when it can so easily be avoided by forewarning employees that the net bonus will be lower than the gross.

Generally, companies will conclude that gain sharing bonuses should not be "benefit-loaded"; that is, bonus payments will not be taken into account when determining income-related benefits, such as savings plans, life insurance, and retirement plans. This means, of course, that any deductions related to these programs would not be withheld from the bonus payment. There are exceptions to this gener- alization, however, and a decision must be explicitly made in advance.

The final concern to be dealt with under the category of payment procedures is the need for a minimum payment provision. It is entirely possible that the gain sharing formula will, in any given period, yield a miniscule bonus pool. If management dutifully divides up the pool and cuts individual bonus checks for the participants, it may find itself distributing ridiculously small amounts (one company once handed out checks for the princely sum of 79¢). This is not the kind of reinforcement that we are seeking, and it probably does more harm than good.

There are two ways to avoid this problem. The more common is to establish a minimum amount that will be paid out. If the gain sharing arithmetic yields an amount that is below that minimum, there is no payout and the pool is carried over to be combined with the next period's pool. Minimum payouts are usually in the $10-$25 range.

The second approach is the variable payout frequency. As described in Chapter 10, this feature requires that the bonus pool continuously accumulate until it reaches a predetermined threshold, say $50,000. Only when this threshold has been breeched does the plan pay out. While the purpose of this provision is normally to ensure that bonuses are paid only when they are quite substantial (rather than simply being "not too small"), it does at the same time eliminate the possibility of minute payouts.

Collective Bargaining Issues

Gain sharing in a unionized organization presents some additional complications, not the least of which are the limitations imposed by the union contract. Two questions typically arise in this connection: should the provisions of the gain sharing system be negotiated and written into the contract, and what is the role of the union if gain sharing is not to be negotiated?

To answer these questions, keep in mind that gain sharing is a non-traditional reward system and, as such, requires a commitment to non-traditional operating practices.

Traditionally, issues have been dealt with in unionized organizations through one of two mechanisms, as depicted in Figure 12-1.

The first of these mechanisms is the collective bargaining process. This process is designed to deal with certain defined issues, among them wages, hours, and working conditions. The bargaining process is adversarial in nature; the two parties sit across the table from each other, have conflicting objectives, and attempt to wield their power to obtain the best possible deal for their constituency. On many individual issues, if not on the entire contract, there is a winner and a loser.

This is not to imply that there is something wrong with the collective bargaining process; it serves a purpose and must continue to exist. But it is basically a win/lose proposition.

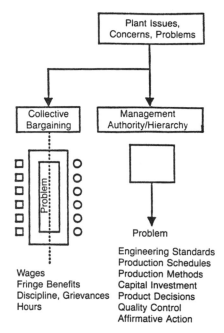

Figure 12-1. Traditional Problem-Solving Vehicles.

Issues that do not come under the purview of the collective bargaining process are handled by the other major mechanism—management authority. Financial decisions, product decisions, scheduling, hiring, and firing are all examples of management prerogative. Decisions made through management authority may or may not be win/lose propositions, but we can expect that there will not be ownership by the union or the rest of the organization for these decisions.

These two decision-making processes—collective bargaining and management authority—have gotten the job done for American industry for many decades. In today's era of international competition and rapid change, however, they are not enough by themselves. A third decision-making process is needed—one in which management and labor can collaborate toward the achievement of goals that are in the best interests of both parties. This additional tool in the organizational arsenal is depicted graphically in Figure 12-2.

This collaborative problem-solving process must not be viewed as a substitute or replacement for one of the other two processes. If it were, management or the union would certainly refuse to participate. It is, rather, a supplement to the traditional processes.

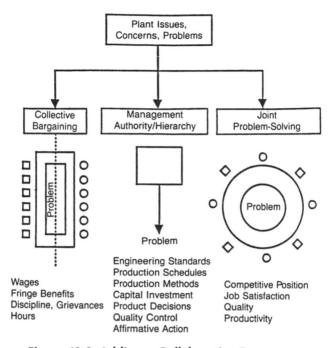

Figure 12-2. Adding a Collaborative Process.

For the collaborative process to succeed, there must be agreement on which issues are appropriate for this process, and management and labor must agree to suspend their traditional adversarial behaviors when addressing these issues. Issues selected are those that will provide a win/win outcome by serving the interests of both parties. Accordingly, there must be no bargaining, for bargaining may not produce the optimal solution to an opportunity which, by definition, serves both parties' interests. The best results can only be achieved through consensus decision making.

Safety is an example of an issue that is a natural for a collaborative problem-solving process. Most management and union people would agree that maximum safety is in both parties' best interest. And collaborative structures to deal with safety, in the form of joint committees, are commonplace in industry. While the collaboration may not always be exemplary in these committees, at least the intent is there.

What is new in recent years is the extension of the cooperative process beyond safety to issues of organizational performance. This is particularly true in industries that have been beset by intense international competition, such as autos and steel. Where survival is at stake, management and union often discover that the improvement of quality, productivity, and other performance variables is in the best interests of both parties and is best served through cooperation rather than conflict.

Cooperative labor/management processes are often organized around employee involvement efforts, as participation and teamwork should certainly qualify as common objectives as well.

Gain sharing is a win/win mechanism if there ever was one. The company benefits through higher performance, increased competitiveness, and improved profitability; for employees, there is higher pay, greater involvement, and increased job security. It is in everybody's best interests to design the most effective gain sharing program possible. This outcome is most likely to be realized through a collaborative design process.

If the design of a gain sharing plan is negotiated, it becomes a bargaining chip. The ultimate shape of the system will be determined by the relative negotiating skills and power of the two parties. Sound design features may be traded away to gain advantage on other contract issues. It will be the product of an adversarial proceeding.

There is another reason why the design of a gain sharing system should not be spelled out in the contract. Gain sharing should be viewed as a dynamic system, subject to modification over time as business needs dictate. These modifications should be made when needed to ensure the continued success and viability of the system. The needed flexibility simply would not be there if the contract had to be reopened every time there was a need to change the system.

The foregoing discussion should not be construed to mean that there should be absolutely no mention of gain sharing in the union contract. In fact, it is probably appropriate and necessary that there be contract language that recognizes and sanctions gain sharing. This language would normally be brief and would simply establish that a jointly designed gain sharing program is not in conflict with the provisions of the contract.

The key point is that gain sharing, as a supporting vehicle for involvement, participation, and teamwork, should be the product of a cooperative design process, the objective of which is to produce a plan that will provide the maximum possible benefit for both parties.

Summary

Any organization planning to install gain sharing must address several organizational, administrative, and compensation issues.

The effect of gain sharing on base pay strategies is one issue that cannot be ignored. While most companies conclude that base pay will continue to be managed in a way that maintains competitive wage and salary structures, others are adopting a "pay-at-risk" approach. The latter strategy can cause some problems but may be necessary for those companies that are facing severe competitive challenges with out-of-line pay levels.

Those companies with traditional incentive programs face an additional complication that must be resolved. While there are certainly exceptions, the predominate trend in industry seems to be toward the elimination of piecework incentives coincident with the launch of a gain sharing program.

The major administrative issue relates to eligibility rules. The status of new hires, terminations, and various absences must be determined in advance. Payment procedures represent another administrative detail; most companies pay bonuses in a separate check and do not "benefit load" the payout.

Finally, the unionized organization must resolve some collective bargaining issues. While there may be some necessary contract language to sanction gain sharing, the design process should normally take place in a collaborative, win/win setting rather than an adversarial contract negotiation.

Chapter 13

Other Non-Traditional Reward Systems

Gain sharing is not, by any means, the only interesting development in the realm of non-traditional reward systems. Today's business imperatives—adapting to ever-changing competitive circumstances, better meeting the needs of the customer, and transforming our traditional cultures—have called into question the effectiveness of virtually all of our traditional reward practices. As Chapter 1 explained, reward system concerns include the following:

◇ The two-class culture created and reinforced by dual pay systems works against the team concept.
◇ Base pay systems that reward employees for specialization and seniority limit the organization's flexibility in deploying its resources and discourage team-oriented work designs.
◇ Merit increase programs are often a sham, as merit may have only a minor impact on the size of an individual's increase.

While gain sharing is a powerful and compelling tool, it alone cannot solve all of our reward system problems. Fortunately, a number of other non-traditional approaches are gaining credence in the United States; three in particular are quite compatible with gain sharing and are worth examining in greater detail.[1]

The All-Salaried Work Force

The differentiation between two classes of employees—salaried and hourly—is a long-established and entrenched feature of reward systems. Most managers give it little thought; it is simply the way things are done.

But many companies today are beginning to ask themselves important questions: What are the hidden costs of a two-class system? Can we expect peak performance from an organization that has an upper class and an under class? How can we convince employees we are a team when we treat people differently?

By classifying its employees into two groups, management clearly confers a favored status on one group. The hourly employee must punch a time clock; the salaried employee is trusted to work the requisite hours. The hourly employee is docked for tardiness and absences; no such penalties are necessary for the salaried employee, who presumably would not take advantage of his employer's trust. Even benefit levels may be different, conferring upon salaried employees a variety of privileges and perks not available to the hourly worker.

Managers are often heard to grouse about the hourly employees' lack of commitment to the organization and its objectives. The fact that the company treats the hourly worker as unreliable, untrustworthy, and a second-class citizen is apparently irrelevant.

Today's competitive challenges require that organizations function as a team, with all employees pursuing productivity and quality improvement with a single-minded purpose. Such a scenario simply may not be realistic in a two-class system.

The solution to this problem, of course, is the all-salaried work force. Every employee is a salaried employee and is therefore presumed to be equally trustworthy. The class distinction is eliminated.

Managers, upon first hearing of the all-salaried concept, typically raise several objections. Surely, they cry, absenteeism and tardiness will skyrocket. The experience, however, is just the opposite—absenteeism often declines in organizations adopting the all-salaried approach. The reason is simple: most people value trust, and when management accords to employees a higher level of trust, they will go to great lengths to avoid violating that trust.

Another common objection is that management will lose a tool to manage those few employees (and there will always be a few) that are irresponsible about working hours. It is interesting to note, as a counterpoint, that they seem to be able to manage that problem among salaried workers (or are all the irresponsible employees in the hourly work force?)

It should be noted that the total elimination of all group distinctions is rendered impossible by legal requirements. The Fair Labor Standards Act mandates that the organization distinguish between "exempt" and "non-exempt" employees, with non-exempt workers receiving a 50% premium for all hours worked in excess of 40 per week. To comply with the law then, management must at least keep track of overtime hours worked by non-exempt employees. But there are no restrictions that preclude us from paying all employees on a salaried, rather than hourly, basis, and therein lies an opportunity to eliminate at least one arbitrary and aggravating distinction.

The all-salaried work force, like the other compensation innovations gaining favor in the United States, is a natural fit for those companies seeking to create an environment where all employees feel a sense of belonging and where employee commitment is high. A substantial number of new plants being built today are designed with an all-salaried compensation system, with such respected companies as Merck, Procter and Gamble, and Hewlett-Packard leading the way.

Merit Bonus Systems

Tying an individual's salary increase to his performance makes eminent sense, but the concept has been so diluted over time that the original intent has largely been lost.

The problem lies, in part, in our practice of using a single vehicle to accomplish, in undifferentiated fashion, several different purposes. The "merit" increase not only rewards the employee for his performance, but is also used to adjust salaries for cost-of-living and other changes in the labor market. Unfortunately, companies often fail to define for the employee the relative impact on his increase of each of these dimensions. Because a significant portion of the increase—the cost of living and market adjustment factors—apply to everyone, it appears to employees that there is actually little differentiation between high and low performers.

Further weakening of the merit concept results from the traditional practice of incorporating the merit increase into the employee's base pay. The merit increase essentially becomes an annuity, as the employee is rewarded for each year's meritorious performance for the rest of his career. Is it surprising, under these circumstances, that longer-term employees may rest on their laurels and serve out their time basking in the benefits of a high salary, swollen by years of merit increases, that bears no relation to their current performance level?

The solution to the merit increase problem is really quite simple: separate the merit portion of the increase from the other components and pay it on a lump-sum basis.

The annual increase then consists of two separate and distinct components. If changes in the cost of living and the local labor market call for, say, a 3% increase in compensation, this amount is awarded across the board and is incorporated into base salaries. Why not, after all, identify it for what it is?

The merit portion of the increase is handled differently. It might range from zero to 15% and, unlike the across-the-board component, is paid in a lump sum rather than added to the base. It is now clear to the employee what his true merit increase is, and most significantly, it must be re-earned every year or it is lost. Resting on one's past laurels becomes costly.

There is also a side benefit to this approach: because an entire year's worth of merit increase is paid in a lump sum, the reinforcement for a job well done is greater. The high-performing employee, upon receiving a check for several thousand dollars, will surely feel that good performance pays.

Any innovation contains potential pitfalls, and there is one here. If the organization's performance evaluation process is not effective, the lump sum approach may not achieve its intended purpose, or worse, may heighten employee dissatisfaction with the reward system. Because the merit increase has much greater visibility and impact, it is important that employees clearly understand what their performance objectives are, how their performance is evaluated, and what behaviors and outcomes lead to higher merit pay. If the performance appraisal process lacks credibility with employees or is not administered properly, the lump sum bonus approach may simply aggravate employee complaints about merit pay.

Several of the Bell System companies have been pioneers in the use of merit bonuses, making use of considerable developmental work done by AT&T prior to the divestiture. BellSouth, for example, instituted a merit bonus system several years ago to deal with a problem faced by many companies with traditional merit programs: employees' salaries tended over time to move toward the maximum for the pay grade, even when performance was not exceptional. Those who reached this high level of pay were there to stay; there was no way to reduce the pay of those whose performance did not justify that level of compensation. In addition, the opportunities to further reward those who truly were top performers were very limited, particularly since a flattening of the organization in the early 80s had significantly reduced promotional opportunities.

The new system installed by the company effectively established a single base pay rate for each pay grade. The base rates change every year based on changes in pay at competing companies. Merit payments for the performance year, on the other hand, are paid in a lump sum and effectively range from zero to 15% of base pay.

As a result, BellSouth's system now differentiates between individual performance through merit payments rather than through base pay. And the potential for differentiation is much greater. Under the old pay system, both the high performer and the low performer would, barring promotions, probably progress to essentially the same pay level. Now, after several years of substantial lump-sum payments, the financial position of the high performer will be considerably enhanced relative to that of his low-performing colleague.

Management reports that this change has focused attention at BellSouth on the issue of pay system effectiveness and has considerably heightened awareness on the part of supervisors of the need to recognize differentials in performance.

The system is not without its problems; as might be expected, the company feels a need to continue to strengthen its appraisal process, which is critical if there is to be effective and credible differentiation among employees.

The merit bonus approach is not as well known and is not yet as widely used as the other non-traditional systems discussed here. But in view of the potential it offers for strengthening the effectiveness of merit pay systems, we can anticipate seeing more of it in the future.

Pay-For-Knowledge

The rapid growth of the team concept in the United States has been noted earlier (Chapter 2). In this non-traditional approach to work design, teams are organized around natural work processes, with every employee being a member of a team. The teams have clearly defined inputs and outputs, performance measures, and goals. Supervisors are trained in participative management, and team building techniques are used to promote cooperation and collaboration among the team members. The team is provided with a greater degree of influence over its work area than is normally found in traditional work systems.

The most advanced form of the team concept is the autonomous, or self-managing, work team. The autonomous work team is accorded almost all of the responsibilities that have traditionally been reserved for supervision. The team sets its own goals and develops its own work schedules. Team members solve problems as a routine part of their jobs. They review each other's performance, handle disciplinary problems among themselves, and hire new team members. The autonomous work team represents a radical departure from traditional approaches to management, but its use is growing and results are impressive.

The team concept works best when employees are cross-trained and capable of performing all of the jobs associated with the team. They then have a much greater appreciation of the overall work process and its interdependencies, and they have greater flexibility in organizing their work. The cross-trained workers typically rotate through the various jobs in order to maintain their skills and to provide greater variety in their work.

An innovation like the team concept requires an innovative reward system to support it. The greater the degree of autonomy accorded to the team, the more critical it becomes to implement cross-training and job rotation. And the more critical it therefore becomes to reward and reinforce the employee's acquisition of multiple skills.

This end is accomplished through a pay-for-knowledge system, also called pay-for-skills or skill-based pay. With traditional systems, an employee's pay is determined by his current job classification or position. Under pay-for-knowledge, in contrast, an employee's pay is determined by the *number* of jobs he is capable of performing. The job that he happens to be doing at any point in time is irrelevant.

The new employee enters the organization at the lowest pay level. As he learns each new skill, and demonstrates proficiency in that skill, he advances to a higher pay level. The highest paid employees, therefore, are the ones that possess the most skills. This is in stark contrast to the traditional approach, where the highest-paid employee is the one holding the highest-skilled position. Under pay-for-knowledge, this employee would be the *lowest* paid, as he is proficient in only one skill.

Pay-for-knowledge systems support the team concept, then, by rewarding employees for obtaining additional skills and therefore enhancing their ability to function as a team.

Pay-for-knowledge, like gain sharing, is a highly flexible system. A large number of skills, for example, can be grouped into skill blocks, with each advance in pay dependent upon the acquisition of all skills within a given block. The system may require that the skill blocks be obtained in a given order, or the employee may be allowed some discretion in choosing his route of progression. In some cases, employees may even construct their own skill blocks by combining skills that have pre-assigned points that reflect each skill's relative difficulty or importance to the organization; each pay increment is then tied to the acquisition of a given number of points.

To ensure that employees have developed a sufficient level of proficiency in a given skill before working on the next one, many pay-for-knowledge plans stipulate that the employee must work a job using a particular skill for a minimum period of time, such as six months, before working towards the acquisition of a new skill. If the needs of the business dictate, the plan may set limits on the number of people who have qualified for a particular skill.

Because increases in pay are tied to the acquisition of skills, it is critical that the organization have an effective and objective means of determining when an employee has achieved proficiency in a particular job skill. This is often accomplished through a means that is entirely consistent with the concept of self-management: proficiency is determined by the employee's peers.

A critical supporting system for pay-for-knowledge is training. If employees are to be provided the opportunity to increase their compensation through the acquisition of skills, the company must provide them ample opportunity to learn those skills. If an employee is prevented from learning a new skill because training is not available, the predictable result will be dissatisfaction and disillusionment with the system. It is incumbent upon the pay-for-knowledge organization, therefore, to make a considerable resource commitment to training.

An often-cited disadvantage of pay-for-knowledge is that it may increase the organization's compensation costs. Because employees can increase their pay through the acquisition of new skills, they typically advance through the various pay grades more quickly than is likely to occur under a traditional pay system. The result is that an employee with a given level of seniority is likely to be earning more than his counterpart in a traditional organization. This disadvantage may be more perceived than real, however, as a pay-for-knowledge organization typically is able to operate with leaner staffing than is a traditional organization, and its employees are invariably more productive when they operate as a team.

While pay-for-knowledge is typically associated with the team concept, it has broader application as well. It is a good fit, for example, for those companies pursuing a job enrichment strategy. As jobs are expanded to include additional responsibilites, pay-for-knowledge reinforces the employee for learning the skills necessary to effectively execute his enriched job.

A Northern Telecom circuit board plant in Santa Clara, California exemplifies the use of pay-for-knowledge to support a high-involvement, team-oriented environment.[2] Prior to 1987, the plant was organized in a traditional fashion, with workers assigned specific, repetitive tasks in a batch production process. In response to the competitive challenges of an international marketplace, the plant was reconfigured into "fast flow lines," a flexible manufacturing concept incorporating just-in-time, kan ban, statistical process control, and total quality control techniques.

Associated with the change in manufacturing philosophy was a complementary change to participative management and the team concept. Employees would be members of flow-line teams, would be multi-skilled, and would practice a greater degree of self-management.

The change to flexible manufacturing and the team philosophy clearly required a change in the plant's compensation system. The acquisition of multiple skills was critical if team members were to understand each processing step, solve technical problems, and reduce waste. Accordingly, a pay-for-knowledge system was installed in 1988.

Each of the plant's six flow lines has ten work stations, such as circuit board preparation, wave soldering, and manual assembly. Each of the ten stations is designated a "skill block," and employees are encouraged to learn all of them. With the acquisition of each skill block, the employee's compensation increases 50¢ to 75¢ per hour. Proficiency must be demonstrated, and employees cannot acquire more than three skill blocks a year.

Results from the flow line and multi-skilled team concepts have been noteworthy: quality (measured by number of defects) improved 63%, and the product delivery cycle has been reduced from four weeks to five days.

Managers sometimes view gain sharing and pay-for-knowledge as an either/or proposition, as if choosing between two incompatible computer systems, Actually, the two approaches serve very different purposes and are quite complementary. Pay-for-knowledge is a base pay system, designed to support the team concept. Gain sharing, on the other hand, is a variable pay system that rewards employees for improving the performance of the organization. There is no conflict between these two objectives; on the contrary, they are mutually supportive.

Well-known companies presently using pay-for-knowledge systems include Procter and Gamble, General Motors, Westinghouse, Cummins Engine, and TRW.

Summary

Gain sharing is not an isolated innovation in the reward system arena. Fundamental changes in the business environment, together with associated changes in management philosophy, compel a fundamental rethinking of our reward system practices. Systems that have served us well for decades may be entirely inappropriate today.

A variety of non-traditional reward systems offers potential for meeting today's business needs. The *all-salaried work force* minimizes class distinctions and thus increases trust and employee commitment to the organization's objectives. *Merit bonus systems* help reposition the merit increase to better serve its intended purpose: reinforcing individual performance. *Pay-for-knowledge* supports the team concept, which represents a major opportunity to achieve an increase in organizational performance but requires a radically different approach to base pay to be fully effective.

These systems are not alternatives to gain sharing; they serve different purposes and are all compatible with the philosophies underlying gain sharing.

References

1. The material in this chapter is adapted from: Belcher, John G., Jr., *Reward Systems: Time for Change:* Houston, TX: American Productivity and Quality Center, 1989.
2. *Case Study 67: Northern Telecom-Santa Clara, California.* Houston, TX: American Productivity and Quality Center, 1988.

Chapter 14

Implementation Strategy

It should be well-established by now that gain sharing is not a simple undertaking. It cannot be designed and implemented quickly with little forethought and planning. Because it offers great potential for fostering and supporting organizational change, it should be done right if it is done at all.

How does an organization do it right? By following a systematic, well thought-out change strategy. Much has been written about change, and the literature contains many useful strategies to implement change. What will be recommended here as a gain sharing implementation plan is a five-step process that is adapted from the classical change strategies.

Our gain sharing implementation strategy consists of the following phases:

1. Exploration
2. Planning and readiness assessment.
3. Preparation for system design
4. System design and plan launch
5. Maintenance and institutionalization

There are of course, no hard and fast rules on how these phases are executed. It should go without saying that the strategy should be tailored to the organization and its business situation. The important thing to remember is that the various steps itemized above are all important to the ultimate success of gain sharing and should therefore be executed carefully and intelligently. The organization should also recognize that proceeding to the next step is always contingent upon a satisfactory outcome in the step before. Lacking that, the process should be terminated or delayed.

Exploration

The initial step in any logical strategy to adopt a non-traditional management process is to obtain a thorough understanding of that process. Before a rational decision can be made about the process, management must be able to clearly answer the following questions:

◇ What is gain sharing, and what is its purpose?
◇ What management philosophy underlies gain sharing?
◇ What are the requirements to make it work?
◇ What are the different approaches to gain sharing plan design?
◇ What have been the experiences of other companies?
◇ How does an organization know if it is ready for gain sharing?
◇ What are the major pitfalls and causes of failure?
◇ How does one design a gain sharing program?

An understanding of these issues is necessary if management is to proceed to the next step. It may well be concluded at this point that gain sharing is not appropriate for the organization at this time, and if that is the case, there is no point in continuing with the implementation strategy.

The vehicles for conducting this exploration are the usual ones:

◇ Readings. There are numerous books and periodical articles available on the subject of gain sharing; the American Productivity and Quality Center's library has about two hundred cataloged. The primary weakness with the current literature is that it tends to focus on the standardized approaches, such as the Scanlon Plan. There is little in the literature on approaches, such as the family of measures, that do not fit neatly into one of the standardized plans. Nonetheless, readings should be a staple of any exploration effort.
◇ Seminars. Educational programs are a natural resource for the exploration phase. Such programs are offered periodically by universities and non-profit business associations. One of the more popular seminars is a regularly scheduled two-day seminar on gain sharing offered by the American Productivity and Quality Center at its Houston facility.
◇ Site visits. Those exploring gain sharing generally find visits to existing gain sharing installations to be helpful. Management tends to draw great comfort from seeing a real gain sharing plan in

action and drawing upon the experiences of others. The union likewise gains confidence in the idea when it is able to see gain sharing plans in action at other unionized facilities. While some companies are reticent to share their experiences with others due to competitive concerns, most welcome the opportunity to talk about their gain sharing successes.

◇ Consultants. An outside expert can be helpful in the exploration phase by providing customized educational programs on site. This mechanism enables all the key players to be educated at once and ensures that they all receive the same information. Because of these benefits, it is often the first major step a company takes. In the interests of obtaining an objective and unbiased education, a consultant selected at this stage should be one who will provide an overview of all the approaches rather than promoting a single type of plan. The consultant should also have an orientation to gain sharing as a change process.

Any company that is seeking to build a collaborative relationship with its union would be well-advised to include the union leadership in this first phase. Their exploration needs must also be met before they can be expected to cooperate in the design and installation of a gain sharing program, and there is no better way to meet these needs than through a joint exploration activity. In addition to raising the union's comfort level with gain sharing, it also models the collaborative process.

Planning and Readiness Assessment

If, after completing the exploration phase, management concludes that gain sharing is worth pursuing further, it must do some strategic thinking. It must determine whether, and how, gain sharing fits with its business strategy.

Any major new process being considered by management should be tested against the company's strategic plan. The business strategy should shape the organization's systems rather than vice versa. And while it would always be advantageous to have motivated and committed employees, some strategies probably preclude that outcome.

Consider, for example, a business strategy that included the following elements:

◇ Cutting costs through work force reductions.
◇ Closing plants and downsizing.
◇ Cutting pay and benefits.
◇ Crippling the union through confrontational tactics.
◇ Tightening controls and centralizing decision making.

This strategy clearly does not rely on the organization's employees for its successful execution. On the contrary, it telegraphs management's attitude that people offer nothing of value to the organization and are expendable.

Gain sharing simply does not fit with this strategy. It can be safely predicted that employees in this organization will have a high level of insecurity, will distrust management, and will fear for their jobs. It would be hard to imagine a less conducive environment for gain sharing.

Now let's look at a different strategy:

◇ Being the high-quality producer.
◇ Increasing responsiveness to customers.
◇ Increasing the skill level of the work force.
◇ Developing a high-involvement culture.
◇ Developing an employment stability strategy.
◇ Forging a collaborative relationship with the union.

This strategy is as different from the previous one as night differs from day. Management here clearly views its employees as critical to its long-term success; employees are viewed as an asset rather than as a necessary evil. There is no philosophical conflict here with gain sharing. As a matter of fact, gain sharing may be necessary to ensure the success of this strategy.

Evaluating gain sharing in light of strategic business objectives is an important step. If the reward system is not congruent with the business strategy, it will, at best, have little or no impact on the success of the strategy. At worst, it will undermine or impede the achievement of business objectives.

Assuming that gain sharing is found to be consistent with the business strategy, management's next concern should be organizational readiness for this non-traditional reward system. More often than not, however, no formal assessment of readiness is conducted prior to the implementation of a gain sharing program. This is unfortunate, as many failures could have undoubtedly been avoided had an assessment been done.

It must be remembered that gain sharing supports a participative management philosophy, and that that philosophy represents change for most organizations. In the best of circumstances, there are many barriers to change which, if not addressed, will undermine the change process. In many cases, the barriers are so severe that the desired change has little chance of succeeding; if so, it would be foolhardy to even proceed.

The assessment of readiness, therefore, should be viewed as a key step in the gain sharing implementation strategy. And the outcome of a readiness assessment should be much more than a simple "go/no go" decision; it should provide objective information about the organization's capacity to support change. By acting on this information, management can then increase the readiness for gain sharing, and therefore its likelihood of success.

In order to conduct a readiness assessment, of course, management must know what organizational characteristics or issues to assess. The key ones, together with the associated questions to be asked, are these:

◇ Management commitment to change. Meaningful, lasting change is unlikely without a high degree of commitment from senior management, for they provide leadership, set the priorities, and control the major organizational systems. Does the top management team at the site under consideration fully appreciate the magnitude of the change required? Is participative management a personal priority of theirs? Are they taking a leadership role in changing the organizational culture? Is their commitment visible to the organization at large?

◇ Information-sharing practices. A high-involvement, high-performance organization cannot exist without open and extensive information sharing. Employees must understand the business priorities, the present performance needs, the customers' requirements, and how their jobs fit in with the overall process. What information-sharing practices and systems are presently used by management? How effective are they? Does management feel the need to increase information sharing? What types of information are not reaching the lowest levels of the organization?

◇ Supervisory receptivity to change. First-line supervisors are key players in any effort to change an organization's style and culture, as they represent the interface between top management and the workers. This level is sometimes highly resistant to change, especially when they do not perceive the change to be of benefit to them and they have not been involved in planning for the change. If supervisors do not support employee involvement, it has little chance for success. What is the present management style of first-line supervisors? Do they seek employee input to decisions? Do they listen to ideas? Have they had any training in participative management skills? How much involvement do they have with their managers?

◇ Present involvement practices. Employee involvement does not just happen. Rather, it generally requires an explicit process and formal structure. What is the history of employee involvement programs at this site? Is there an effective involvement process in place presently? Do employees feel that their ideas will receive fair consideration? What are future plans for increasing the level of involvement?

◇ Level of teamwork. Traditionally, jobs have been designed around individuals, and organizations have been structured functionally. The turf protection and the lack of common goals that often result are detrimental to performance and represent impediments to the effective functioning of a group reward system such as gain sharing. To what degree do the various departments or functional groups cooperate with each other? Do employees have a sense of being part of a team? Is greater teamwork an explicit objective of management?

◇ Level of trust. Low trust between employees and management represents a major impediment to a successful gain sharing program. Employees will be skeptical of management's motivations and will suspect hidden agendas. They also may not trust the numbers that are reported, fearing management manipulation to reduce the bonuses. Do employees generally believe that management is open with them? Do they feel that they can count on management to follow through with their commitments? Do people feel they have been treated fairly in the past?

◇ Union receptivity to change. Union resistance to employee involvement and gain sharing dramatically increases the risk of failure. It may be impossible to even implement a non-traditional reward system in this circumstance. Union resistance typically stems from either a distrust of management or a high level of discomfort with deviating from traditional union principles. Is the union-management relationship adversarial or cooperative? Has there been a recent history of conflict? What is the position of the union leadership on gain sharing and employee involvement? Are the union leaders receptive to non-traditional union roles?

◊ Employment stability. If employees fear for their jobs, they are less likely to support gain sharing, partly because they will fear that any productivity improvements made will result in work force reductions and partly because they will doubt that management is sincere in wanting to develop a participative culture. What is the history of layoffs and work force reductions? Do employees feel secure in their jobs?

◊ Business situation. If declining business activity is in prospect, the time may not be propitious for gain sharing. Management will be distracted, retrenchment may be necessary, and performance improvements will be hard to come by. By the same token, if major changes—restructuring, significant new product introductions, major technology changes, acquisitions or divestitures—are in the offing, the associated turmoil and the invalidation of past performance measures may wreak havoc on the gain sharing system. What are the short-term prospects for the business? What major product, business, or structural changes are anticipated in the near term?

Having identified the readiness dimensions to be investigated, attention should now turn to the assessment process. How does management obtain the information necessary to make sound decisions with regard to readiness?

The first issue that must be dealt with here is whether this information should be obtained through internal resources or through the use of an external consultant. The answer to this question is situational; if the requisite skills are present internally and management is confident that the internal resource can obtain objective information and is willing to provide objective feedback to management, then simple economics would dictate that the internal resource be used. The principal advantages of an external consultant are that he may be able to elicit more candid information, will not be as constrained by political considerations, and will have well-developed diagnostic skills.

The next process issue is how the necessary information will be obtained. There are two basic approaches: the cheap, quick-and-dirty way, and the right way.

The cheap-and-quick way is simply to have management evaluate themselves. How do they answer the questions outlined in the list of readiness issues discussed earlier? There is no free lunch, of course, and there is a major trade-off for this cheapness and quickness. The trade-off is that the information obtained will be biased and therefore suspect.

Invariably, management's perspective on these issues is at least partly at variance with reality. The problem stems largely from poorly developed lines of communication and organizational politics. Senior management tends not to receive complete and accurate information from the working level, partly because they do not take the time to seek it and partly because there are effective buffers in the form of intervening layers of management. The information that gets through these buffers tends to be highly filtered and incomplete. A highly developed sense of self-esteem and a natural inability to be totally objective about oneself also contribute to this biased viewpoint.

If one wants to do a serious readiness assessment, it is imperative that information be gathered from all levels of the organization. Only then can an objective picture of the status of the key readiness issues be obtained.

There are three primary vehicles for obtaining readiness data from a cross-section of the organization:

◇ Written surveys. The survey is the first assessment instrument that comes to mind, and most organizations have conducted surveys at various times in the past. The classic attitude survey, however, will normally not provide sufficient information to judge the organization's readiness for gain sharing. This traditional form of survey simply does not zero in on some of the key readiness issues, such as management commitment to change, supervisory receptivity to employee involvement, and union support for gain sharing. A survey that is tailored specifically to gain sharing readiness issues, of course, is another matter and may prove quite useful. In any event, the principal advantage of the survey approach is that it enables data to be gathered from a large number of people at relatively low cost. The major disadvantage is that survey data is rather sterile and must be interpreted. Quantitative survey data lacks richness and provides little insight into the true dimension and causes of poor communications, etc.

◊ Individual interviews. Confidential, one-on-one interviews with a cross-section of employees represent the other end of the spectrum of assessment vehicles. The interview format has advantages and disadvantages that are the opposite of those of the survey. In contrast to the survey, interviews are time-consuming and allow input to be obtained from only a limited number of employees. On the other hand, interviews provide robust, detailed information about the various readiness issues. A skilled interviewer can explore subtleties, seek examples, and obtain clarification.

◊ Group processes. A variety of small-group data-gathering techniques, such as group interviews and focus groups, represents a useful middle ground between the written survey and the individual interview. Group processes allow greater numbers of people to be involved than is possible through individual interviews, yet at the same time provide richer, more qualitative data than can be obtained through surveys.

A useful case study of a multi-site readiness assessment is provided by the U.S. Foods Group of The Pillsbury Company. Group management recognized that gain sharing offered an excellent opportunity to support employee involvement in the company. Having no prior experience with gain sharing, however, there was a desire to carefully select the site for initial implementation. The author was engaged accordingly in 1989 to assess the readiness for gain sharing at 19 plants.

In the interest of completing this project in a cost-effective and timely fashion, information gathering was limited to one day at each plant site, using the following vehicles:

◊ Three individual interviews with senior management.
◊ Two focus groups with hourly employees.
◊ One focus group with first-line supervisors.
◊ One group interview with union leaders in organized plants.

Participants in the focus groups were selected to provide a reasonable demographic cross-section of the work force. The group process was highly structured to ensure full participation and was designed to provide both quantitative data (such as would be obtained through a survey) and qualitative information about each of the readiness dimensions.

Feedback to management included all of the comments obtained (anonymously, of course), a summary of the quantitative responses, and the consultant's conclusions regarding the positive readiness characteristics and the readiness concerns for each location. The outcome of the project was the immediate selection of a pilot site and the commencement of a gain sharing design process at that location. A side benefit was that all plants now had data regarding their climate and involvement practices that could be of considerable value in planning the course of change.

One of the better examples of an internally conducted readiness assessment is provided by Armstrong World Industries, the flooring and building products manufacturer. A management task force was established at Armstrong in 1989 to develop the broad specifications for a pilot gain sharing program for the company. Once that task was completed, the task force developed a readiness assessment process to evaluate and select the pilot site. Members of the task force personally conducted the assessment through management interviews and employee focus groups.

The Armstrong assessment explored the status of six major readiness criteria, with some divided into sub-categories:

1. Employee involvement
   ◇ Employee involvement approach and deployment
   ◇ Teamwork
   ◇ Training practices/plans
   ◇ Union receptivity to past changes and to explore gain sharing
   ◇ Employee receptivity to past changes and to explore gain sharing
   ◇ Supervisory support of involving employees in process improvement
   ◇ Trust
2. Business situation
3. Leadership
   ◇ Top management demonstrated leadership
   ◇ Demonstrated ability to change
4. Information sharing and communications
5. Compensation system
6. Performance measures

The specific questions asked for each of the criteria are detailed in Appendix A.

The readiness assessment, of course, should not be limited to those situations where a pilot location must be selected from among a number of candidates. Even where only a single site is under consideration, a readiness assessment will generate important information about potential barriers to the success of a gain sharing program.

Assuming that the readiness assessment does not reveal any fatal impediments, and management is comfortable that they can deal with the issues that surface, the organization is ready to proceed to the next step.

Preparation For System Design

It has been stressed before that the design of a gain sharing system is a critical success factor. It can make or break the system. It is vitally important, therefore, that it is done right. An organization must have an effective design process, and it must provide adequate time to do the job properly.

In preparation for the design effort, management should address the following issues:

◊ Nature of the design process
◊ Timing and resources
◊ Management guidelines/requirements

Nature of The Design Process

The first question is, should a consultant design the system for us, or should we do it ourselves? The best answer is almost always the latter: Do it yourself. This does not mean that there is no legitimate role for a consultant. In fact, a consultant who is thoroughly familiar with the design options and pitfalls can be invaluable. The proper role for a gain sharing consultant, however, is to *facilitate* the design process. There are two problems with having the consultant design the system:

◊ He cannot know the business, the culture, and the organizational history as well as management and employees do. He may well design a system that does not meet the business needs, that is perceived as inequitable, or is flawed in some other fashion.

◊ He will feel a strong sense of ownership for the system, but no one else will. The system will have to be "sold" to the rest of the organization.

Assuming that the system is to be designed internally, the next question is, who should be involved? The traditional answer would be to assign the task to an individual or to a committee of managers. But why would an organization want to take a traditional approach to the design of a non-traditional system that is intended to support a non-traditional management philosophy?

In the interest of greater employee involvement (which is, after all, a major objective of gain sharing), the system should be designed by a team of management and non-management employees. Including people at all levels in the design process will ensure that the resulting system meets the needs of both the business and employees and is perceived as equitable. It will also provide a degree of ownership for the system that is unobtainable otherwise.

The ideal design team would be selected to meet the following criteria:

◊ Representation from all major functional groups or departments.
◊ Representation from all levels—middle-management, first-line supervision, non-management salaried and hourly employees.
◊ Members are thoughtful, team-oriented, and will be active participants.
◊ Members are informal leaders, respected by their peers.

In considering the size of the design team, a trade-off must be weighed. A large design team would provide significant benefits in terms of more involvement and more ownership, but would be unwieldy and could find it hard to reach consensus on design issues. A small team can be efficient and effective, but would limit the direct involvement opportunity. Most design teams have between six and twelve members, a range which probably provides for a reasonable balance between the trade-off issues.

One way to involve a larger number of people without seriously hampering the team's ability to function is to make use of sub-committees. A large team (perhaps 15-20 in number) could assign its members to serve on various sub-committees, each with a small number of members. Sub-committees could be formed around such issues as the formula, the baseline, the share-frequency-split, the treatment of capital investments, and employee involvement mechanisms. Most of the work would be conducted in these sub-committees, which would make recommendations for approval by the full committee.

Allocation of Time and Resources

The design of a gain sharing plan involves a sizeable number of decisions, with several options for each. The options must be carefully weighed to ensure equity, a good fit with the business needs, and consistency with other design decisions. Data will need to be gathered to facilitate some decisions, and simulations of the system should be run. All of this takes time.

A good rule of thumb is that an effective design process will require six months, with the design team meeting weekly. Forcing the work to be done to a tighter deadline increases the risk that the design will be flawed, and a flawed design in turn increases the risk of failure. Given the importance of gain sharing to long-term business objectives, does it make any sense to short-cut the design process by two or three months?

To some extent, the time requirement is dependent upon the nature of the system being designed. A profit-sharing plan is relatively simple from a design standpoint and could likely be accomplished in somewhat less than six months. The family of measures approach is normally the most time-consuming to design; six months probably represents a minimum reasonable target in this case.

The major resource requirement, apart from the cost of a consultant, is the time of the design team members. Clearly, they must be prepared to devote a significant amount of time to this effort, which wil detract from the time available to perform their regular jobs. If management is not willing to support this time commitment, the job will not get done properly.

Management Guidelines/Requirements

While the detailed design of the gain sharing plan will be left to the design team, management should provide some guidelines to this group for two reasons. First, the potential approaches are so varied that the design team may well flounder in trying to sort through them and reach a decision. To the extent that management has some predilection toward a specific structure, this preference should be communicated to the design team in order to narrow the field and enable the group to obtain focus without undue delay. Management may want a profit-sharing plan, for example, or they may favor a family of measures with an emphasis on quality and customer satisfaction indicators. Some articulation of general parameters such as these will facilitate the timely execution of the design process.

Second, there may be certain specific design features that management deems to be requirements if the plan is to be approved. Examples of such requirements that have been mandated in actual design efforts include:

◇ A site-inclusive group
◇ A baseline that changes in some fashion at least annually
◇ A mechanism to ensure that large bonuses are not paid out in times of low profitability
◇ A provision for capital investment adjustments
◇ A distribution mechanism that meets the requirements of the Fair Labor Standards Act without requiring retroactive over-time pay adjustments

If, indeed, management has certain requirements relative to the design of the plan, they should be communicated to the design team up front rather than hoping that they will come up with the "right" answers. If they don't and management rejects the plan, time will have been wasted and the design team will be deflated.

Management guidelines and requirements can go too far, of course. They can be so detailed and limiting that they remove a great deal of the design team's discretion and undermine the whole point of having the gain sharing plan designed by the participants. But it is certainly reasonable for management to narrow the options somewhat and to establish certain requirements that they believe to be critical to a successful plan design.

System Design and Plan Launch

With a design team in place and properly charged by management, the design process can begin.

An important first step in that process is to educate the design team on the fundamentals of gain sharing, including its definition, purpose, and design components. Assuming that the design team is an organizational cross-section, as suggested earlier, it is unlikely that all of the members have had a great deal of exposure to gain sharing. Asking these people to make intelligent decisions about a complex system like gain sharing without the benefit of education on the subject is foolhardy.

At a minimum, the design team should attend an educational workshop conducted by an internal or external person who is knowledgeable about the subject and can present an objective, balanced overview of the options for each of the design components. The design team's educational agenda might also include readings and site visits.

In addition to gain sharing education, it is often useful to conduct some team-building exercises as well. The team members may have had little prior experience with team decision making and probably lack team skills. Even a minimal appreciation of the basics of team behaviors and consensus decision making can go a long way toward increasing the effectiveness of the team's deliberations. Because of the importance of a good group process, these teams are often provided with a trained facilitator to serve as a permanent member of the group.

It can also be helpful for the design team to develop a charter to guide their deliberations. The Bushings and Bearings Division of J.P. Industries, a transportation components manufacturer headquartered in Ann Arbor, Michigan, initiated a gain sharing design process at their plant in Caldwell, Ohio in 1990. The effort was structured as a joint labor-management process, with the design team consisting of representatives from both management and the United Steelworkers of America.

To guide this collaborative effort, the design team developed a charter that spelled out what they expected to accomplish and how they would work together. The charter is reproduced in Appendix B.

There are two other process issues that the design team should consider before taking on the technical design issues. One relates to obtaining input from the rest of the work force. While the purpose of a cross-sectional design team is to provide for participant input, even broader input would further increase organizational ownership for the system. At a minimum, the organization at large should be kept informed of the design team's discussions and conclusions as the design process unfolds. These communications serve to limit speculation and rumors, increase the employees' understanding of the gain sharing program, and serve as the basis for seeking input to issues presently under consideration.

Design teams usually meet this need through either the distribution of meeting minutes or the publishing of a newsletter devoted exclusively to gain sharing. Design team members should also be encouraged to seek input from their peers regarding the issues presented in the communications vehicle.

The second process concern relates to communications with the management decision makers. Waiting until the design process is complete before presenting the team's work to the approval authorities is a mistake, particularly if the people in question are physically located elsewhere and do not have normal, routine contact with the design team members.

When the person who must approve the gain sharing program sees the system design for the first time in its completed state, there is a high probability that he will have serious misgivings about the design. He has not been privy to all the discussion that has transpired around the design components and therefore may not fully appreciate the rationale behind various design decisions. Furthermore, he may have his own ideas (which he unfortunately has failed to communicate) about how things should be done. He may also be aware of business constraints or management initiatives that should impact the system design but which are not generally known. If, for whatever reason, the decision maker sends the design team back to the drawing board, the consequences can be serious. Much time has been wasted by the design team members going down the wrong track, and the high degree of ownership that they feel for the system has been severely undermined.

The solution to this problem is to keep the approval authorities informed of design decisions on a regular basis. If senior management is uncomfortable with the direction of the design team around any particular issue, this input can (and should) be provided early in the process rather than at the end. Design team members can then make their case or change direction before they have locked in their decision. Ideally, the approval process at the end of the project should be largely ceremonial, as senior management already understands, and has bought into, the system design.

With their education and team-building needs met, and having made provision for on-going communications upwards and outwards, the design team is now prepared to tackle the technical design issues. Before reaching any decisions, of course, the team should thoroughly review the various options and ensure that there is a true consensus among the team members.

To ensure that the design issues are addressed in the proper order and that no important steps are overlooked, the design team might follow a work plan such as this:

◊ Define the participating group or groups. The group component (Chapter 4) is logically the first one to address, as many of the other design issues are dependent on this decision. The team cannot, for example, make an intelligent decision about the formula until it knows who the gain sharing participants are. A meaningful formula for one group might be totally inappropriate for another group.

◊ Select a basic formula structure. Does the organization want a physical productivity formula, a financial formula, or a family of measures (Chapter 5)? The answer to this question is dependent upon the business objectives, the state of the involvement process, the sophistication of the work force, the position of the union, the time allocated for the design process, the input of management, and a few other things as well.

◊ Itemize the costs/variables to be included. If the team has decided on a physical productivity formula, this step is essentially accomplished; the variable to be measured is productivity. If it has selected a financial formula, on the other hand, it needs to define what types of costs will be included—will the plan measure only labor costs, or will it include a variety of costs? If the latter, which costs? If the formula category selected is the family of measures, which variables will be included? Productivity, quality, material utilization, schedule compliance, customer satisfaction, attendance, and safety are all examples of variables that are commonly found in the family of measures approach. This step is best accomplished through a brainstorming and ranking process of some kind.

◊ Identify specific measures or sources of data. If labor productivity is on the list, how is it presently measured? If the team is pursuing a multi-cost ratio that includes eight cost elements, where does it get data on those eight costs? If quality is to be an element in the system, what are the various indicators of quality? It is desireable, of course, to use existing measures if at all possible.

◊ Gather historical data for each of the measures under consideration. Ideally, obtain three years of history, by month. If three years is unavailable, get as much as possible. This step obviously must be done outside of the design team meeting.

◊ Graph the history, by month and quarter. This is an important step that is often overlooked by untrained design teams. These graphs will be invaluable in making several design decisions and will enable the team to avoid many pitfalls. As an illustration, look back at Figure 9-1. The different historical patterns depicted in this graph should lead plan designers to different conclusions regarding an appropriate baseline. These patterns will be difficult to discern without a graphic depiction of the measure's history. These graphs will also clearly show the degree of volatility of each measure; this information will be useful when considering the need for a smoothing mechanism later. Finally, the graphs will readily show any aberrations in the data, which may reflect either unreliable data or measures that are susceptible to sudden variation. In either case, the use of the measure in question may need to be reconsidered.

◊ Establish baselines. The measures that have survived to this point have a high priority of making the final cut, and now the question of baselines should be considered. The design team must ponder the issue of historical versus target baselines (Chapter 9) and, lacking any guidelines from management, choose between these two basic options. Having disposed of that issue, the specific baseline value must be determined. What historical period should be used, or what should the target actually be? The answers will be found through the application of good judgment, common sense, and a sensitivity to the needs of both the company and the participating employees. If the design team has chosen the family of measures as its basic formula structure another question will predictably arise: must all of the measures have consistent baselines? While such an outcome would be beneficial, it should not be forced if it is unrealistic or would damage the credibility of the system from either a management or employee point of view. The baseline for each measure should be justifiable and stand on its own merits.

◇ Establish rules for baseline changes. What will happen to the baselines in future periods? Will the baselines ratchet, roll, or remain fixed (Chapter 9)? If they are not to remain fixed, what is the precise arithmetic that will govern their change? Deferring or ignoring this issue will almost surely lead to problems later. Here again, the appropriate answer will only become apparent through team discussion and consideration of business needs.

◇ Determine method of valuing gains. If gains are to be shared, there must be a means of quantifying those gains. In some cases, it may be quite straightforward; the multi-cost ratio (Chapter 7), for example, provides for its own valuation. In other cases, the solution is not so easy. How much is an improvement in safety worth? How about an increase in customer satisfaction? Often, it is possible to analytically derive a value; costs associated with lost time and workmen's compensation could be considered, for example, when attempting to value a safety measure. The result may not be perfect, but a reasonable approximation should suffice. For some measures though, an analytically derived value may be next to impossible to achieve. In these situations, the value will need to be somewhat arbitrary. For cxample, $5,000 could be added to the bonus pool for each percentage point increase in customer satisfaction as measured by a survey. The fact that the accountants cannot identify the precise financial gains in this case should not be allowed to stand in the way of progress.

◇ Simulate the system. This represents another important step that is easy to overlook. The design team should forecast the likely improvement in the measure or measures and calculate the payout that would result. In fact, several simulations should be run, perhaps one each for a minimal improvement, the likely level of improvement, and the maximum expected improvement. The purpose of these simulations is to test the outcomes for reasonableness. If the simulations suggest that only very small bonuses are likely, the design team needs to go back to the drawing board, for the system as designed is not likely to stimulate sufficient employee enthusiasm. Likewise, if very large bonuses appear likely, the team can anticipate great apprehension from the management quarter. This does not mean the system is not viable, but it may mean that some modifications, such as a lower employee share, are called for in order to obtain management approval. With a personal computer and spread-sheet software, the design team can easily play many "what if" games, trying out different baseline and share assumptions as well as a variety of different improvement projections. These simulations are well worth the effort, as they will greatly increase management's comfort level with the final system design.

◊ Finalize employee share, payout frequency, and distribution decisions. The remaining mandatory design components should now be disposed of, if they have not been already. A review of Chapter 10 will define the options and criteria for these decisions, which, like everything else, should be based on team consensus and should reflect business needs and considerations of fairness.

◊ Consider the need for a smoothing mechanism. Chapter 11 pointed out that a smoothing mechanism (deficit reserve, rolling payout, etc.) may be critical to the long-term viability of a gain sharing program. The design team should first consider the need for such a feature, given the volatility of the measures and the frequency of the payout, and then select the best option to meet the need, if there is one.

◊ Consider the need for capital investment adjustments. Chapter 11 also discussed the rationale for providing a means to adjust the baseline for gains associated with major capital investments. If such a provision is deemed necessary (some input from senior management may be needed here), the team must decide the threshold level of capital investment required to trigger an adjustment, the mechanics of the adjustment, and the timing of the adjustment. As was suggested earlier regarding the baseline change issue, this decision should not be overlooked or a price may be paid later.

◊ Determine eligibility requirements. It will be recalled from Chapter 12 that simply defining the boundaries of the group does not relieve us of any further concerns about eligibility for gain sharing bonuses. It may be appropriate that certain members of the participating group—new hires, terminations, leaves, etc.—be excluded from receiving a bonus in a given period. All of the possibilities need to be considered and appropriate provisions written into the plan.

◊ Develop plan maintenance procedures. Gain sharing plans should be dynamic instruments, evolving over time to adapt to ever-changing business conditions and the dynamics of continuous performance improvement. This issue will be discussed in depth later under the final phase in our implementation strategy—Maintenance and Institutionalization. Suffice it to say here that procedures to perform regular plan maintenance should be developed and written into the plan prior to its implementation.

◇ Develop education/communications strategy. Employee understanding and buy-in to the gain sharing program is essential to its success. To achieve these ends it is necessary to devise an effective strategy to educate the organization on the purpose of gain sharing, the specifics of the plan design, and the role of employees in bringing about improvements. This activity is important enough that the design team should not consider its task completed until it has developed a plan for its effective execution.

◇ Plan for employee involvement structure to handle ideas. The point has repeatedly been made that gain sharing is an enabling mechanism for employee involvement. Unless a company is relatively advanced in its involvement process, it may lack adequate mechanisms to handle employee ideas for improvements. This state of affairs will work to the detriment of gain sharing, as the participants' inability to have their improvement ideas heard, evaluated, and implemented will lead to frustration and lack of support for the program. What good does it do for employees to have gain sharing if they have little or no influence over how things are done in their work area? The design team therefore should carefully consider various mechanisms (or evaluate the effectiveness of existing ones) for handling employee ideas. There are a variety of options, including simple suggestion systems, departmental suggestion committees, brainstorming sessions, task forces, and problem-solving teams. Because employee involvement drives performance improvement, the design team must not shortchange this issue.

◇ Plan the launch. As a final step, the design team should ensure that all the ducks are lined up in a row. What is the launch date? Will the necessary approvals be in place? How and when will the education of the work force take place? What changes need to be made to the payroll system in order to accommodate the issuance of bonus checks? Does accounting have all of the inormation it needs to adjust its bookkeeping and financial reporting activities? It is clearly desireable that the launch go smoothly and that there be a minimum of last-minute hassles and glitches.

Key to a successful plan launch is an effective and well-executed education/communications strategy. The major objective, of course, is to ensure that all participants understand the gain sharing system and know what they have to do in order to earn bonuses. A second objective is to create a sense of anticipation and enthusiasm for the program.

The communications plan should include a variety of elements. It will certainly include a written document of some kind that will spell out the details of the gain sharing plan. Many companies have invested in professionally printed brochures or booklets for this purpose. It will also likely include face-to-face meetings with employees to present an overview of the plan and to answer questions. Some organizations create logos for their gain sharing programs and use them in various ways to maintain visibility and awareness of the program. Other communications media, such as slide shows, video tapes, and posters can also be used effectively.

The communications strategy should also include appropriate mechanisms for communicating plan results on a regular basis. A fundamental element of any involvement process is feedback; people need to know how they are doing and why. Feedback not only provides reinforcement for positive results, but also provides information that can be used to problem solve and generate improvement. It is not enough that employees simply know what their bonus was for a given period; they should also receive thorough explanations of why the numbers turned out the way they did.

Maintenance and Institutionalization

The launch of the gain sharing program does not complete the implementation process; the system must be managed and maintained on an ongoing basis. The failure to do so represents a final pitfall that must be avoided.

Unanticipated problems will likely arise, and these must be dealt with in a systematic fashion if the system is to continue to function effectively. In addition, the business needs will change over time and the gain sharing program must evolve as well or it will become irrelevant. There is no place in a dynamic business environment for a static, inflexible system, particularly one that has a major influence on employees' behavior.

There are a variety of legitimate reasons for changing a gain sharing program:

◇ There is a design flaw that results in an inequity from either a company or employee point of view.
◇ The system is too complicated for employees to understand.
◇ There is little improvement opportunity left in a given measure.
◇ A major change in product/service lines or technology has taken place.
◇ The business strategy changes.
◇ Employee commitment to the business has increased to the point where more of a "common fate" orientation is appropriate.
◇ The program simply isn't working.

While frequent and constant changes in the gain sharing system are not desireable, it would be folly to allow the system to fail because it could not be changed in a fair and timely fashion when it needed to be. The best vehicle to accomplish these changes is a management/employee steering committee. Analogous to the design team, this committee would be a multi-level, cross-functional group. Its role would be to manage the gain sharing process on an ongoing basis.

More specifically, the steering committee's activities would likely include the following:

◇ Reviewing the payout data each period and communicating these results to the work force.
◇ Ruling on questions of plan interpretation, such as the eligibility of an individual whose situation is not clearly addressed in the plan provisions.
◇ Ensuring that employee ideas for improvement are being handled in a timely fashion.
◇ Conducting an in-depth review of plan results and problems on an annual basis.
◇ Recommending changes to the plan, as needed.

The use of a steering committee to manage the plan serves the same objectives as did the employee design team: fair decisions and employee ownership for plan changes. It is entirely consistent with the employee involvement philosophy that gain sharing is intended to support.

Ultimately, of course, we would like gain sharing to become institutionalized. We would like it to be an integral element of organizational functioning, firmly embedded in the culture, as much a part of the compensation system as base pay.

To reach this destination will take years and possibly many revisions to the gain sharing program. But once there, employee involvement and continuous improvement will be ingrained to a degree that is probably unachievable otherwise. And an organization with these characteristics will surely be a high performer by any standards.

Summary

Given the non-traditional nature of gain sharing and its importance in supporting organizational change, a careful and systematic implementation strategy is called for. The starting point is *exploration,* through which management and other key stakeholders in the organization become familiar with the basics of gain sharing: the philosophical underpinnings, the variety of possible approaches, and the keys to success. The next logical phase is *planning and readiness assessment,* during which management considers the fit of gain sharing with the company's business strategy and evaluates the readiness and capacity of possible pilot locations to support change. *Preparation for plan design* entails selecting a design team and allocating time and resources. During the *system design* phase, the design team develops the detailed plan provisions, including an effective communications strategy and the necessary administrative support procedures. Finally, there is an ongoing *maintenance and institutionalization* phase, which ensures that the gain sharing plan evolves to meet changing business conditions and ultimately becomes a permanent and integrated element of the corporate culture.

Chapter 15

Summing Up

Before ending our review of gain sharing, it would be wise to look at the major causes for failure of some gain sharing programs. The cumulative experience of hundreds of companies over the past decade or so has clearly identified several major forces that have been responsible for gain sharing failures, and any company considering this non-traditional reward system should be aware of these forces. With a little thought, of course, one could probably surmise by now what these pitfalls are. Nonetheless, it would be well worth our while to summarize the failure causes, as a small number of them account for a sizeable proportion of the gain sharing failures.

To close on a more positive note, our second task will be to summarize the key principles of this book.

Causes of Failure

Any long-time observer of the gain sharing scene will likely be struck by the fact that companies seem to make the same mistakes over and over again; gain sharing programs that fail can usually be attributed to one (or more) of a handful of causes. If management did nothing more than ensure that these deadly forces were not operative, the probability of success with gain sharing would be extremely high.

Not surprisingly, some of the key causes of failure are related to the readiness issues discussed in the previous chapter. Others can occur even in the most ready environment.

Lack of management commitment to change. It has been emphasized repeatedly in this book that gain sharing is a non-traditional reward system that supports a non-traditional management philosophy. Unfortunately, traditional processes and practices are entrenched in the vast majority of business enterprises. While employee involvement and teamwork are growing, their level is often miniscule by the standards of what could be.

Too many managers fail to view gain sharing as an agent of change. They install gain sharing because (a) they think everyone will work harder if a carrot is dangled in front of them, or (b) other companies are doing it, so it must be a good thing. They fail to appreciate that the organization's traditional (that is, autocratic and control-oriented) mindset gives rise to an array of powerful forces that will ensure that employees are not empowered to make the contributions that will generate the desired gains.

If gain sharing is to succeed in the long run, management must be prepared to attack these forces. They must work to overcome employee mistrust, the lack of meaningful participation, supervisory and middle management resistance, poor information sharing practices, job insecurity, and a variety of other detrimental factors. If these forces are allowed to run rampant, they will slowly but surely eat away at the fiber of the gain sharing system.

It is important to reiterate here that these issues should not be addressed solely for the sake of gain sharing. They should be attacked because they represent major inhibitors to *business performance*. If management is not prepared to take a leadership role in changing the organization's culture, gain sharing will be no more effective than any of the countless other failed programs that have preceded it.

The importance of *union commitment to change* should also be emphasized as a corollary to this principle. Many of the changes that must take place also strike at the heart of traditional union principles, and a union orientation toward maintenance of the status quo is just as deadly as a lack of management commitment to change.

Lack of an effective employee involvement process. While commitment to change is a necessary ingredient, it is not sufficient by itself. The organization should actually be doing something substantive in terms of employee involvement.

This does not mean that the organization must be a model of a high-involvement system, with self-managed teams and no traditional forms of supervision. It does mean that gain sharing should not be the *first step* in an employee involvement process. If the organization has not significantly increased its information sharing, has not provided even a modicum of training in participation skills, and has not had at least some success with basic involvement techniques, it is not likely to have a positive outcome with gain sharing. To repeat a phrase used earlier, you cannot buy employee involvement through gain sharing.

Clearly, the farther the organization has traveled down the road to change, the more likely it is to have success with gain sharing. At some point however, further progress on the journey will likely become dependent upon a supportive and congruent reward system.

Poor system design. Anyone who has read Chapters 3 through 11 on the gain sharing design components should have a healthy appreciation for the complexities of a gain sharing system. Failure to appreciate these complexities and to think carefully through the system design represents a major cause of failure.

Design-related failures usually result from one of two causes: (1) there was an attempt to force-fit an inappropriate system, either because management attempted to copy a success in another organization or a consultant sold a predetermined design; or (2) the system designers did not carefully think through the design options and the implication of their decisions. The result is an unanticipated (and usually negative) outcome that undermines the credibility of the system from either a management or employee point of view.

Low or nonexistent payouts. A gain sharing program that pays little or nothing for an extended period of time is at risk of collapsing. This is particularly true during the early part of the program's life, when the system is unproven and its existence is fragile.

A lack of payout may result from setting baselines that are too difficult to reach, or it may simply be a matter of poor timing. Launching a gain sharing program at the beginning of an economic downturn is risky, as it may be difficult to improve certain gain sharing measures in the face of declining business volume. A different timing problem was encountered by a company that implemented gain sharing immediately prior to the start of an ongoing organizational restructuring. The costs associated with the restructuring ensured that gains would be impossible to come by through the early life of the system.

Low payouts may also be a symptom of low readiness; the lack of an effective involvement process may severely limit the organization's ability to generate gains.

Conventional wisdom holds that a gain sharing program should have the potential of paying at least 3-4% bonuses to have the necessary motivational impact. As discussed in the previous chapter, simulating the system to ascertain the payout potential is an important step in the design process.

Failure to properly educate employees. A high level of readiness and a well-designed gain sharing system do not by themselves guarantee success. Employee must also have a basic *understanding* of the system and their role in improving the measures. The education/communication process must be done well; it is not enough to simply throw together a handout and distribute it without further explanation.

When employees fail to understand the gain sharing system, several problems can be expected:

◊ A lack of clarity on what types of improvement will be rewarded.
◊ An inability to relate gain sharing to specific job functions.
◊ Little appreciation of what must be done differently in order to earn bonuses.
◊ Skepticism about reported results.

The investment of the time and resources necessary to adequately educate employees will significantly enhance the chances of success with gain sharing.

Basic Principles of Gain Sharing

Certain themes have been recurrent through this book.

First of all, this book is about *change*. The business environment has changed dramatically over the past decade, as countries around the world have become tough competitors. The emergence of a global economy has exposed hidden weaknesses in the American approach to management. Flat or declining productivity, poor quality, and bureaucratic organization structures have rendered many of our companies, even entire industries, uncompetitive.

In seeking a response to this problem, American industry has discovered that people can make a difference. In fact, many would argue that any company that hopes to survive must have a reasonable level of commitment and involvement from its employees. Surely, any organization that aspires to being "world class" must pursue the high-involvement model.

Obtaining this involvement, however, requires fundamental change in management philosophy and practices. Long-standing assumptions about the role of employees, job design, information sharing, and management control must be challenged and ultimately changed.

If the necessary cultural change is to be effected, the issue of reward systems cannot be ignored, as rewards have a major influence on behaviors. Reward systems designed in a different era, under a different set of management assumptions, will not get the job done. Of the variety of non-traditional reward systems available to support change, gain sharing perhaps offers the greatest promise, as it directly rewards employees for their contributions and can be adapted to any business process or work structure.

A second major theme is that gain sharing should be treated as a *supporting system* rather than as an end in itself. It may seem like a paradox, but gain sharing is probably least effective when it is positioned as the driver for improvement. When gain sharing, rather than employee involvement, is the focal point for the improvement process, the participative practices that are necessary to make gain sharing work will probably not be established. People improve organizational performance when they are empowered to do so; no amount of reward can overcome a lack of empowerment.

A third major theme is that gain sharing works best when it is *customized* to the needs of the organization and the business. Gain sharing systems have slowly but surely evolved from a small number of standard plans to an infinite variety of designs. Adopting a standardized approach without considering the opportunities for customization surely represents a lost opportunity for most organizations. Customization requires extra time and effort, of course, but the payback is a more effective system that meets the business and organizational needs.

Furthermore, a gain sharing plan should be viewed as a dynamic system, adapting to the ever-changing needs of the business. The use of a standardized design would limit the organization's ability to innovate in response to changing strategies and marketplace demands.

The formula offers the greatest opportunity for customization and reflection of different pay philosophies. Formulas can be constructed to reward performance variables that are highly controllable by employees, or they can provide variable pay based on market forces and business results. In addition, formulas are no longer limited to basic measures of productivity and cost. Service levels, timeliness, customer satisfaction, and employee involvement are all legitimate variables for today's gain sharing programs.

Opportunities for customization are not limited to the measures, however. Rolling baselines, variable shares, dual frequencies, and segmented pools are all examples of creative ideas that can be found in today's gain sharing systems.

Summing up, one thing is clear to this observer: if American business ever needed real employee involvement, it needs it now. It is not an option; it is a business imperative. Survival through the 90s and into the twenty-first century may well depend upon it.

Any company that believes this to be true cannot ignore the issue of rewrds. Expecting employees to have a greater commitment to the business and to make ever greater contributions to the success of that business without a reward system that reflects that commitment and contribution is too high an expectation.

Gain sharing supports that need, meets that business imperative. It is a system whose time has come.

Appendix A

Armstrong World Industries Assessment Questions

Employee Involvement

I. Employee Involvement Approach and Deployment
   A. Has employee involvement been initiated in any areas of the plant? If so, describe where and how employee involvement is being used.
   B. Describe the problems encountered with employee involvement.
   C. What is the next phase of employee involvement for your plant? How do you plan to get there?
II. Teamwork
   A. What efforts has the plant made to improve informal teamwork and cooperation on the job?
   B. To what extent are formal teams being used to further continuous process improvement?
III. Training Practices/Plans
   A. List the type of training that is available and conducted at your plant (salary and hourly) and estimate the percent of the plant population that has received this training.
   B. Who is responsible for training follow-up and how is its effectiveness evaluated?
   C. What are your future plans for training?
IV. Union Receptivity to Past Changes and to Explore Gain Sharing
   A. How would you characterize the union-management relationship here?
   B. Give examples of how the union has reacted to major changes that have taken place over the last three years that have affected them.

    C. Has the union agreed to modifications of contractual language or past practice in order to facilitate improvement efforts?

V. Employee Receptivity to Past Changes and to Explore Gain Sharing
    A. How would you characterize the hourly employee-management relationship here?
    B. Give examples of how the plant's employees have reacted to major changes that have taken place over the last three years that have affected them.

VI. Supervisory Support For Involving Employees in Process Improvement
    A. What percent of the time do supervisors spend:
        ◇ Coaching
        ◇ Training
        ◇ Administrative
        ◇ Fire Fighting/Handling Problems
    B. Describe the supervisor's role and authority in dealing with idea handling mechanisms (ECR's, suggestions, opportunities for improvement, etc.).
    C. How have supervisors demonstrated their commitment to employee involvement?

VII. Trust
    A. How would you assess the present level of trust between employees and management?
    B. Has the level of trust improved within the past two years? If so, to what do you attribute the improvement?

Business Situation

I. Are there any major changes planned in the following areas and if so, what?
        ◇ Capital Improvements
        ◇ People/Organization Changes
        ◇ Product or Process Change
        ◇ Growth/Decline in Business

II. What are the biggest challenges presently facing this plant?

Leadership

I. Top Management Demonstrated Leadership
    A. Describe plant management staff involvement in planning, designing, giving, and receiving training.

B. How is management modeling employee involvement behavior?
C. How do you establish strategies/objectives and communicate them to the entire organization?
II. Organization's Demonstrated Ability to Change
   A. Describe all of the major changes involving the plant in the last three years.
   B. Do you have documented "plans" for future changes? If so, explain.

Information Sharing and Communications

I. Describe present information sharing practices. How effective are they?
II. Describe the types of information currently shared with *ALL* employees.
III. What changes have you made to information sharing/communications within the past two years?
IV. List the information below that your plant won't share with *ALL* employees.

Compensation System

I. Describe your short-term and long-term compensation strategy.
II. Are existing incentives effective in meeting plant objectives and goals?
III. Would existing incentives present a conflict with a gain sharing plan?

Performance Measures

What has been the trend in the following performance measures over the last 2-3 years?

Category	Measure
Material	Scrap-Percent
Productivity	Unscheduled Downtime
	Process Effectiveness-Percent
Quality	Claims-Actual Plant Responsibility
Service	Product Cycle Frequency-Percent
	Finishing Schedule Adherence-Percent
	1. Family Schedule Adherence
	2. End Item Schedule Adherence
	On Time Shipments-Percent

Flexibility   Set-Up Time Key Operations
Safety   Number of Recordable Injuries/100 Employees
                     Number of Lost Time Injury Cases/100 Employees
                     Number of Days Away from Work/100 Employees

Appendix B

J.P. Industries
Gain Sharing Design
Team Charter

I. *Team Purpose*

To design a plan that provides the opportunity for all employees to share in the financial gains resulting from improvements made through their involvement.

II. *Major Team Responsibilities*

A. Design a plan that is consistent with the employee involvement process, strategic objectives, manufacturing processes, employee capabilities, accounting systems, communications practices, market place conditions, and existing improvement opportunities.

B. To make design decisions through consensus decision making and not through negotiations, popular vote, or other means.

C. To develop an effective communications process that keeps all employees informed of the plan development.

D. To present to Company Management and representatives of the Local and International Union a proposed gain sharing plan to include recommendations as to the status of the current incentive systems.

E. To present to all employees the plan for their approval.

III. *Major Objectives*

The major objective is to make the following design decisions and establish policies and procedures.

A. Designation of the group to which the gain sharing plan applies.

B. A formula through which group performance is measured.

C. A baseline against which improvements in the formula are compared.

D. A share arrangement, or basis for dividing the gains between the organization and its employees.

E. A payout frequency.

F. A payout distribution method to allocate the employee share of gains to individual employees.

G. A deficit reserve to reduce to some degree the risk to the organization.

H. Employee involvement structures to provide the means for employees to bring about the gains.

I. A means of adjusting the formula or baseline for major capital investments made by the organization.

J. The status of the current incentive system.

Index

L

Labor costs, as gain sharing
measure (*see* Costs and Labor
Productivity)
Labor-management cooperation
(*see* Unions)
Labor productivity, as gain
sharing measure, 42,44,
45-46,50,73,83-86
Lawler, Edward E., III, 24
Lennox Industries, 39
Lincoln Electric, 6
Losses, effect of, 123-124
Loss recovery (*see* Smoothing
mechanisms)
LTV, 42-43

M

Maintenance, plan, 180-184
Material utilization, as gain
sharing measure, 31,38,
42,73,83-86,97
McGraw Edison, 53
McGregor, Douglas, 22,60-61
Measures (*see* Formula)
Mead Corp., 39
Merck, 154
Merit pay
gain sharing, relation to,
138
lump-sum payments for,
154-156
problems with, 4,9,37,154
Miami Paper Corp., 77-79
Minimum payout, 146-147
Mix adjustments (*see* Product
mix, adjusting for)

Mobay Chemical, 37-38
Modifiers, 87,90-91,111-113
Motorola, 10,23-24,70-72,113,140
Multi-cost ratio, 60,66-68,
73-75,77-78

N

Northern Telecom, 159
Nucor Corp., 41-42,139

O

O'Dell, Carla, 49
Overtime, effect on bonus
distribution, 117-118

P

Participants in gain sharing (*see*
Group, participating)
Participative management (*see*
Employee involvement)
Part-time employees (*see*
Eligibility for gain sharing)
Pay-for-knowledge (*see*
Pay-for-skills)
Pay-for-skills, 5,21,156-160
Pennsylvania, University of, 25
Pentair, Inc., 77-79
Phillips Petroleum, 53
Piecework (*see* Incentives,
individual)
Pillsbury, 39,169-170
Pitney-Bowes, 53
Prestolite, 53
Price effect, elimination of, 56,
66,76,77
Procter & Gamble, 154,160

readiness for gain sharing,
impact on, 166-167
United Auto Workers, 69
United Brotherhood of
Carpenters and Joiners,
67
United Steelworkers of
America, 60,175
United Auto Workers (*see*
Unions)
United Brotherhood of
Carpenters and Joiners (*see*
Unions)
United States General
Accounting Office, 15
United Steelworkers of America
(*see* Unions)

V

Value added, 63-66
Variable compensation,
8-9,46-47

Volatility of measures,
114,123-124

W

Walton, Richard, 22
Weighting (*see* Product mix,
adjusting for)
Westinghouse, 160
Wharton School, 25

X

Xerox, 24,79-81,118,140

Y

Yield (*see* Material utilization)